GU00792199

# IN SEARCH OF BYRON
# IN ENGLAND AND
# SCOTLAND

A GUIDE BOOK

by

Anne Fleming

1988

Old Forge Press · Ditchling Press

i

1988

Published by

OLD FORGE PRESS

and

DITCHLING PRESS LTD

ISBN 0 9513010 0 4

ISBN 0 9500584 4 0

Set in Century Old Style
Printed in Great Britain by Ditchling Press Ltd, Sussex

*Books of travel are expensive and I don't want them*
Byron

iii

# CONTENTS

BYRON IN SCOTLAND                                    Page
Gight Castle (ruin) .....................................................  3
Haddo House ...........................................................  4
Fyvie Castle ...........................................................  4
Aberdeen ...............................................................  5
Banff ...................................................................  9
Deeside ...............................................................  10
Loch Leven ...........................................................  11
Abbotsford ...........................................................  12

BYRON IN ENGLAND
Newstead Abbey .....................................................  17
Annesley Hall .......................................................  18
Hucknall .............................................................  21
Nottingham ...........................................................  23
Thrumpton Hall .....................................................  24
Southwell ............................................................  25
Newark on Trent ...................................................  26
Melbourne Hall .....................................................  28
Matlock Bath .........................................................  29
Chatsworth ...........................................................  29
Peak Cavern ........................................................  30
Cambridge ...........................................................  30
Brighton ..............................................................  34
Bowood House .....................................................  36
Bath ..................................................................  39
Cheltenham ..........................................................  40
Eywood (ruin) ......................................................  41
Castle Howard ......................................................  43
Seaham ..............................................................  44
Alnwick Castle .....................................................  47
Flodden Field .......................................................  48

BYRON IN LONDON

| | Page |
|---|---|
| Harrow School | 51 |
| House of Lords | 52 |
| 50 Albemarle Street | 53 |
| St James's Street | 53 |
| St James's Palace | 54 |
| Bennet Street | 55 |
| Piccadilly | 57 |
| Theatre Royal Drury Lane | 61 |
| Royal Opera House, Covent Garden | 62 |
| Holland House, Holland Park | 62 |
| Melbourne House, Whitehall | 65 |
| Westminster Abbey | 66 |

## APPENDIX

SOME PAINTINGS AND PRINTS OF BYRON'S PERIOD

| National Portrait Gallery WC2 | 69 |
|---|---|
| National Gallery WC2 | 70 |
| London Museum EC1 | 70 |
| Victoria and Albert Museum SW7 | 70 |
| Sir John Soane's Museum WC2 | 71 |
| The British Museum WC1 | 71 |
| The Scottish National Portrait Gallery, Edinburgh | 71 |
| The Prints and Drawings of Byron's Period | 72 |

AT THE TIME OF GOING TO PRESS THE TIMES GIVEN FOR OPENING OF HOUSES ETC. AND ALL OTHER INFORMATION ARE CORRECT BUT THEY SOMETIMES CHANGE AND SHOULD BE CHECKED. TELEPHONE NUMBERS ARE GIVEN FOR THIS PURPOSE.

# ACKNOWLEDGEMENTS

I am most grateful for advice and assistance in preparing this book from the following:

Mr Michael Rees, Vice President of the Byron Society; Mrs Beatrice Hanss, who is infinitely generous with her wide knowledge of the Romantic poets; Miss Lucy Edwards, M.B.E., who knows all there is to be known about Byronic Nottinghamshire; Mrs Gwen Beaumont who has done valuable research on Byron in Nottingham; Mrs Joan Pierson, who has done valuable research on London; Mrs Megan Boyes; Mrs Dorothy Kirkham; Mrs Barbara Jackson (all of whom belong to the Byron Society); Ms Pamela J. Wood of Newstead Abbey; Ms Suella Postles and Ms Haidee Jackson of the Castle Museum, Nottingham; Mr Robert Jenkins of the Arrow Bookshop, Kington; Ms Monica Anton of Banff; Ms Margaret Davidson of Banff; Ms Gillian Edwards of Cambridge; Mr Frank Goddard of Cuckfield; Mr S. C. Morrison of Ruislip; Mr Stan Thornton of the Theatre Royal, Brighton; Mr Jacob Simon of the National Portrait Gallery; Mrs Barbara Milner of the Victoria Gallery, Bath; Mrs Joyce of the Reference Library, Bath; Dr Steven Blake of the Cheltenham Art Gallery; Mrs Catherine Williams and Mrs Jennifer Milgrove of City of Aberdeen Art Gallery; Mrs M. I. Anderson of Aberdeen University Library; Westminster City Libraries Archives and Local History Department; English Heritage; The Local Studies Department of the Public Library at Kirkby in Ashfield; the staff of the tourist office at Kincardine and Banchorie; the Rev. N. C. Heavisides of Seaham; Mr John Wilson Groves; Major R. P. Chaworth Musters; Mr Eeyan Hartley, Archivist at Castle Howard; Mr Peter Day, Archivist at Chatsworth; Dr Shrimpton, Archivist at Alnwick Castle; Mrs Weston of Melbourne Hall; Mrs Gowans of Fyvie Castle; Mr Macrombie of Aberdeen Grammar School; Mr Jim Waugh of Haddo House.

Some of the information on St James's Street came from the *Survey of London*, The Athlone Press, University of London.

Some of the information on Piccadilly came from *The Ghosts of Piccadilly*, an entrancing book by G. S. Street, Archibald Constable, 1907.

# BYRON IN SCOTLAND

*. . . My heart flies to my head,*
*As Auld Lang Syne brings Scotland one and all,*
*Scotch plaids, Scotch snoods, the blue hills and clear*
*streams,*
*All my boy feelings, all my gentler dreams.*

Statue of Byron in front of the present Aberdeen Grammar School,
the work of the sculptor poet Pittendrigh Macgillivray.
Reproduced by kind permission of *Aberdeen Journals*.

## RUIN OF GIGHT CASTLE, ABERDEENSHIRE

Ordnance Survey Landranger maps are used throughout. Gight Castle (Sheet 30, Grid Ref. 83/39). Take the B90095 from Ellon through Methlick. A rough road to the left leads through Stonehouse Farm and on, to the ruin of the Castle, which stands on the brink of a rocky slope looking down towards the Braes of Gight.

*I am half a Scot by birth and bred a whole one.*

The name Gight means a windy place. Byron described the castle as—

*All tenantless save to the crannying wind.*

It was built on the L plan. The kitchens had a large fireplace and a huge chimney. There was a vaulted bakehouse and cellars. The walls were enormously thick. The hall was on the first floor and measured 37 feet by 21. The castle was sacked by the Covenanters in 1644.

The Gordons of Gight were Byron's maternal ancestors:

*My mother was precise on points of genealogy like all the Aristocratical Scots. She had a long list of ancestors—like Sir Lucius O'Trigger—most of them to be found in the old Scottish Chronicles—in arms and doing mischief.*

The Gordons of Gight descended from the Stuart Kings, and Lairds of Gight since 1490 were a wild race who killed and were killed in a series of horrific events: foray, murder, siege and battle. The 13th and last Laird was Catherine Gordon who went south to Bath in 1795 and there met Captain John Byron who was a widower in search of a second heiress to finance his expensive way of life. They married in Bath and lived at Gight where he drank her whisky and danced to the music of her pipers. Soon he had gambled away her fortune. There was an old saying:

'When the herons leave the tree
The Lairds of Gight will landless be.'

When the Third Earl of Aberdeen saw the herons come flying south to Haddo House from the Gight heronry he said 'Let the birds be for the lands will soon follow'. A year later he bought Gight for his son, Lord Haddo, for the sum of £17,850, most of which went to Mad Jack Byron's creditors. The Gight heiress was reduced to living on an income of £150 a year. Her husband continued to sponge on her. They fled to France from his creditors but she returned to England for the birth of her son. Within two years she had brought the child to live at

3

Aberdeen. Lord Haddo was killed at the age of 27 in a riding accident at Gight.

Byron wrote to his friend, Douglas Kinnaird, years later, from Italy, to say that he would like to buy back Gight Castle from the Earls of Aberdeen, even if it meant a loss of income.

## HADDO HOUSE, ABERDEENSHIRE

Haddo House may be reached from the B999, 20 miles north of Aberdeen and from the A981, 10 miles north of Oldmeldrum. Admission May to September, every day from 2 p.m. to 6 p.m., except May Day weekend. Tel. (06515) 440. Light Refreshments in the Stable Building.

Haddo House is a magnificent classical building designed by William Adam in 1731.

The Earls of Aberdeen were descended from Jock of Scurdargue, a natural cousin of Elizabeth Huntly whose son was created the First Earl of Huntly. The Gordons of Methlick and Haddo were therefore kinsmen of the Gordons of Gight, who were descended from the Second Earl of Huntly and Princess Annabella Stuart.

In the house are several portraits of politicians known to Byron or satirised in the poetry: in the Anteroom are portraits of the Duke of Wellington, Sir Robert Peel, Pitt the Younger and Lord Castlereagh as well as the Fourth Earl of Aberdeen who offered to put Byron up for his newly founded Athenian Club. In the Dining Room is a portrait of the actor, John Philip Kemble. On the staircase is the portrait of Lord Haddo painted in Rome when he was on the Grand Tour, by Pompeo Batoni.

## FYVIE CASTLE, ABERDEENSHIRE

Off the main Aberdeen to Banff Road, the A947. Signpost to Fyvie Castle in the village of Fyvie. Admission—1st May to 30th September, daily, 11 a.m. to 6 p.m. Last admission 5.15 p.m.

A small Tea Room in the Victorian Kitchen provides sandwiches and home baking. Tel. (06516) 266.

4

*My mother was as haughty as Lucifer with her descent from the Stuarts and her right line from the old Gordons, not the Seton Gordons, as she disdainfully termed the ducal branch, always telling me how superior her Gordons were to the southern Byrons notwithstanding our Norman and always masculine descent.*

Fyvie is a magnificent 13th century castle with 5 towers and a very fine wheel stair. It was a royal stronghold in mediaeval times and the land around it was a royal hunting forest. King Robert the Bruce held an open air court of justice in the beech woods here.

The connection of Fyvie with Byron pertains to the history of the Gordon family. The Second Earl of Aberdeen, William Gordon, married Lady Anne Gordon, daughter of the Second Duke of Gordon. They lived at Fyvie. When Lord Aberdeen died in 1745 he left Haddo to his eldest son, George, now Third Earl of Aberdeen, and Fyvie to his nine year old son, the Hon William Gordon. In the drawing room is the famous 18th century portrait of William Gordon painted at Rome by Pompeo Batoni.

The tower to the north of the wheel stair is known as the Gordon Tower.

Byron's great grandparents, Alexander Gordon of Gight and Margaret Duff Gordon, are buried in the graveyard of Fyvie Church among the graves of the Gordons of Fyvie.

---

## ABERDEEN

*To meet an Aberdonian was at all times a delight to me.*

The little boy who might have been brought up in feudal grandeur at Gight Castle, neighbour to Lord Aberdeen, served by his own people and pipers, presiding over the yearly Gight Games, when the prettiest girl was dubbed the Rose of Gight, lived instead in an apartment in Broad Street, Aberdeen. This was no bad thing, for Aberdeen provided him with influences that affected his whole life. Aberdeen first formed his ideas on books, politics, war, and love, and instilled into him a certain superstition that he never quite lost, a love of the sea, a love-hate relationship with religion:

*I deny nothing but doubt everything,*

and the common touch—an ability to get on with all sorts of people without a hint of patronage.

Mrs Byron lived at first in Queen Street and then moved to Broad Street not far from the harbour. As a small boy Byron could wander about the harbour and learn about ships and ship building and the smell and sound of the sea. Later he could ride by the shores of Aberdeen Bay. His poetry is full of images of the sea:

*In the wind's eye I have sailed and sail, but for*
*The stars I own my telescope is dim,*
*But at the least I have shunned the common shore*
*And, leaving land far out of sight, would skim*
*The ocean of eternity. The roar*
*Of breakers has not daunted my slight, trim,*
*But still seaworthy skiff.*

He swam in the Don and learned that, although he was lame, when he was in the water he was equal to boys with two perfect feet. He learned not to fear the sea and this explains his calmness during later adventures when he found himself in peril at sea. During the last voyage to Greece a storm broke away the stalls which had been set up for the horses below decks. Several horses were galloping about in the dark in terrible confusion. Byron went in and calmed them down, an act of extraordinary courage.

ABERDEEN MARITIME MUSEUM, PROVOST ROSS'S HOUSE, SHIPROW
Admission. Monday to Saturday, 10 a.m. to 5 p.m. Tel. (0224) 50086.
This is Aberdeen's oldest building and must have been familiar to Byron. The museum deals with fishing, whaling, shipbuilding, wrecks and rescues, and the development of the harbour.

ABERDEEN GRAMMAR SCHOOL, SKENE STREET
The Grammar School Byron attended from the age of 7 was in Schoolhill. It is the oldest in the British Isles, established about 1256. A fine modern statue of Byron by Pittendrigh Macgillivray, stands in the courtyard of the present building.

JAMES DUNN'S TOWNHOUSE, 61 SCHOOLHILL
Admission. Monday to Saturday, 10 a.m. to 5 p.m.. Tel. (0224) 646333.
This is an 18th century town house, renovated for use as a museum

for special exhibitions. James Dunn was Rector of Aberdeen Grammar School in Byron's time.

PROVOST SKENE'S HOUSE, QUESTROW, OFF BROAD STREET
Admission. Monday to Saturday, 10 a.m. to 5 p.m. Tel. (02245) 50086.
Tea, coffee, and light meals are served in Provost Skene's Kitchen. This is a 17th century furnished house with period rooms and displays of local history. Byron must often have walked past it as a boy.

### THE MARISCHAL COLLEGE, BROAD STREET
The Marischal, though rebuilt since Byron's time, still stands a little further down Broad Street than the house, long gone, where Mrs Byron lived with her 'wee cruikit deevil, Geordie Byron'. The porter said, after Byron's death, that he 'minded well' the little boy in the red jacket and nankeen trousers he was always having to chase out of the yard. Mrs Byron employed two tutors from the Marischal to get her son into the Grammar School. He was a heedless student but once he could read he read voraciously. Mrs Byron subscribed to one of the three circulating libraries in Aberdeen. There were several booksellers including Brown of the Homer's Head.

### CASTLEGATE
Here the old Mercat Cross is still standing with the tall Tolbooth Tower nearby, both familiar sights for the young Byron. In Castlegate, known as the Plainstones, Aberdonians would promenade, talking of politics and plays, of fashion and trade, of the departure of the whaling ships and the arrival of regiments of Volunteers. Here the young Byron watched military parades: *My earliest dreams were all martial.* Such dreams led him to boast:

*I will, some day or other, raise a troop of men which shall be all dressed in black and ride on black horses and they shall be called Byron's Blacks and you will hear of them performing prodigies of valour.*

When he grew older and wiser he took a more sensible view of military matters:

*There are ways to benefit mankind as true,*
*Perhaps, as shooting them at Waterloo.*

At the Plainstones he would have seen the latest copy of the *Aberdeen Journal* being passed from hand to hand when exciting news from

France arrived concerning the Revolutionary Wars and the rise of Napoleon. Mrs Byron had been brought up a Whig and she was liberal in her politics. She said of the French Revolution, 'I do not think the King, after his perjury and treachery, deserves to be restored. To be sure there has been horrid things done by the people but if the other party had been successful there would have been as great cruelty committed by them.' Later, Byron echoed this sentiment:

> . . . *I wish men to be free*
> *As much from mobs as Kings, from you as me*

In Castlegate lived the little girl who was his first love, Mary Duff, his cousin. They met at the dancing class in Peacock's Close and Byron, aged 7, fell madly in love. Later he thought it very odd that he should have been so devoted to her at an age when he could neither feel passion or know the meaning of the word.

## BRIG O' BALGOUNIE

Byron is known to have felt superstitious fear when riding his pony over the steep cobbled carriageway of Brig o' Balgounie which is still standing near the crook of Don not far from the new Bridge of Don. The old bridge is a beautiful stone structure with tall pointed arch and great buttresses, with deep dark pools below. Byron was the only son of his mother and he knew the verse of Thomas the Rhymer which went:

> 'Brig o' Balgounie,
> Wight is thy wa',
> Wi' a wife's ae son,
> And a mare's ae foal,
> Down shalt thou fa'.'

The grown Byron was superstitious. He was afraid of the dark. He also dreaded his 36th year as he had been told that the years 1816 and 1824 would be dangerous for him. The Brig o' Balgounie may be still standing but 1816 was the year of Byron's downfall and 1824 the year of his death.

Brig o' Balgounie can be reached by walking through Seaton Park and down to the river path. On the way you may see the Wallace Tower (1616) which has been transferred from Netherkirkgate where it was in Byron's day. He talked of it years later in Venice.

The Bridge was a two-mile ride for Byron on his pony from Broad Street. On the way he would have passed through Old Aberdeen.

8

Passing along College Bounds and High Street, Byron would have ridden past King's College with its Crown Tower and Chapel, the Georgian Old Town House, the Chanonry, and St Machar's Cathedral, which stands high on a ridge with its twin spires overlooking the crook of Don. The High Street still has many 18th century houses with the old Mercat Cross standing on the west side. Several small streets leading off from the High Street have been restored: Don Street, Grant's Place, Cooper's Place and Wright's Place, all give an idea of what Old Aberdeen must have looked like in Byron's day.

## BANFF, BANFFSHIRE

The county town of Banff stands north west of Aberdeen at the mouth of the River Devoron on the Moray Firth. To approach it one takes the A947 and enters the town by way of the seven-arched Banff Bridge, as Byron and his mother did when they visited Mrs Byron's grandmother, Margaret Duff Gordon of Craigston, at her house, Little Fillicap, on the site of the present Sherriff House. The town is built on a hill and there are still rows of mediaeval, 16th, 17th and 18th century houses arranged in terraces and steep narrow streets above the water. Banff Castle is at the top, on Castle Street, the Mercat Cross on Low Street near the site of Mrs Duff's house. South of Low Street is the Gardens thought to be the site of a Carmelite Monastery. Nearby in Waterpath was the Manse where Byron visited his kinsman, the Rev Abernethy Gordon. The Manse Garden is thought to have been the Abbott's Garden. Here Byron played one of the pranks that gave him the name in Banff of 'the young English Nickom'. Byron told the story to Pryse Gordon in Brussels in 1816. He had climbed a tree in the Minister's garden to get at some pears on a wall and had tumbled down:

*The Minister's wife blabbed to my mother and the old red-nosed Doctor was sent for who insisted on bleeding me in spite of screams and tears, for I was a complete spoiled child. He produced the lancets, of which I had a complete horror, having seen them used to bleed my nurse, and I declared that if he touched me I would pull his nose. He gave the bleeding up, condemning me to be put to bed and fed on water and gruel.*

9

Byron threw the medicine out of the window and his mother gave him bread and butter instead of *brochan.*

(Years later he was less successful in fending off the efforts of the doctors to use their lancets on him. During the terrible death-bed scenes in Greece he kept them off for six days, but then gave in. "In my weak state", he said, "bleeding will inevitably kill me." And so it did.)

The *Annals of Banff* relate that a visitor to the Manse who knew Byron's daughter, Lady Lovelace, was told the story of Byron and the pears and sent her some fruit and grafts from the tree. It is possible that descendants of Byron's Pear Tree, as it was inevitably called, are to be found at Ockham.

The restored 18th century house known as Brandons is thought to have belonged to Mrs Catherine Abercromby of Birkenbog, a sister of Mrs Duff Gordon. This lady remonstrated with Mrs Byron in the presence of the 7 year old Byron whereupon he butted her like a ram with his head and threatened to throw her over the balcony.

### DUFF HOUSE
Beside the Golf Course, south of the Gardens.
Admission. April to September, Monday to Saturday, 9.30 a.m. to 7 p.m. Sunday, 2 p.m. to 7 p.m.. Tel.(02612) 2872.
This is the Georgian baroque mansion of the Earls of Fife designed by William Adam. Margaret Duff Gordon was a cousin of the First Earl of Fife. Byron would have been familiar with the house as a boy.

## DEESIDE, ABERDEENSHIRE

From Aberdeen the A93 takes you through this region to Braemar and Inverey. Take the south Deeside Road, the B796, from Aboyne.

*And Lochnagar with Ida looked on Troy,*
*Mixed Celtic memories with the Phrygian Mount,*
*And Highland Linns with Castalie's clear fount.*

### BALLATERACH FARMHOUSE
Here, Byron was sent to *drink goat's fey after a threatened decline after the scarlett fever in 1795.* The farmhouse has been rebuilt but still stands on the same site, south of the B796, midway between Dinnet

and Ballater. (Sheet 44, Grid Ref: 42/96). The 8 year old boy wandered over this countryside, resplendent in his Gordon tartan.

Here you may see the grave of Mary Robertson, the second daughter at the farm, who was the 'Mary' of *'When I roved, a young Highlander'*. (He was a very young Highlander indeed at the time—no more than eight years old.)

To the west of Braemar is the village of Inverey and a mile beyond it is the bridge leading to the Linn of Dee. (Sheet 43, Grid Ref: 6/90). There Byron walked with his gillie, slipped and almost fell in the wild waters below. There was no bridge at that time.

Lochnagar is south of Balmoral Forest (Sheet 44, Grid Ref: 25/85). A good view of it may be had from Loch Muick. Follow the road south from Ballater through Glen Muick past the Linn of Muick to Spittal of Glenmuick. Walk from there to Loch Muick from which there is a fine view of Lochnagar (3,786 feet).

Byron wrote that he *climbed thy steep summit, Oh Morven, of snow* and he related that Morven was recalled to his mind years later when he saw the wild mountains of Albania. Drive from Ballater via Crathie to Lary and go on through Glen Morven to the site of Morven Lodge (1,350 feet). From here a rough track, for walkers only, leads two and a half miles across open country to the summit, gradually climbing the remaining 1,500 feet. From the summit (2,862 feet), Deeside can be seen to the south, Lochnagar to the south west, the Grampian mountains to the west, and Culblean Hill (1,983 feet) to the south east.

If you decide to rove over this mountainous country you will need a weather forecast and stout shoes and should ask advice during the deerstalking season (August to October).

# LOCH LEVEN, KINROSS

Captain John Byron had returned to France and died there in 1791.

In 1798 came news that the Fifth Lord Byron was dead. The ten year old boy from Aberdeen was heir to Newstead Abbey and wide lands in Nottinghamshire. Mrs Byron sold all her furniture to pay for the journey south. It fetched £72. They left on the 4 a.m. Aberdeen to Edinburgh fly and passed by Loch Leven where Mary Queen of Scots made her famous escape.

## ABBOTSFORD, MELROSE

Sir Walter Scott's house, on the banks of the Tweed, is on the B6360 between Melrose and Selkirk.
Admission. From 3rd Monday of March to 31st October from 10 a.m. to 5 p.m. daily. On Sundays from 2 p.m. to 5 p.m. Tel. Mrs Maxwell Scott, O.B.E. (0896) 2043. There is a teashop.

Byron never went to Abbotsford but he admired Sir Walter Scott as poet, referring to him as the Ariosto of the North, and when Stendhal criticised Scott's character, Byron defended him warmly:

*I have known Scott long and well and in occasional situations which call forth the real character . . . of all men he is the most open, the most honourable, the most aimiable. . . . I say that Sir Walter Scott is as nearly a thoroughly good man as man can be, because I know it from experience to be the case.*

Abbotsford is full of historical relics collected by Scott: Rob Roy's gun, Montrose's sword, Prince Charlie's quaich. There are 9000 rare books in his library. Among these objects is a large silver urn filled with bones—the Athenian skulls Byron brought home from Greece and later presented to Sir Walter Scott. Scott in return presented Byron with an ornamental Turkish dagger. In the collection is also a ring with a lock of Byron's hair which Scott wore. In the private apartments is a print of Byron which Scott kept hanging in his room.

Byron had satirised Scott in *English Bards and Scotch Reviewers* but later repented of his youthful savagery and apologised for it. Scott was magnanimous enough to forget this completely. After Byron had been hounded out of the country he wrote a favourable review of *Childe Harold Canto IV* defending Byron's character. At that moment this took great courage and Byron never forgot it.

HADDO HOUSE
Reproduced by kind permission of the National Trust for Scotland
from the Trust's Haddo House Guidebook.

13

BYRON AGED 17. PORTRAIT MINIATURE 1805
Augusta Leigh wrote 'This miniature of my poor brother was the best taken and given to me on my birthday.'
Reproduced by kind permission of Newstead Abbey, Nottingham Museums.

## BYRON IN ENGLAND

In 1816, Byron was hounded out of England by rumour and scandal. He found this hypocritical. The morals of Regency England were atrocious. The only sin that counted was to be found out.

*In England the only homage they pay to virtue is hypocrisy.*

A year later, he could write:

*England! With all thy faults, I love thee still!*

and from exile he could still claim:

*Yet was I born where men are proud to be, not without cause.*

## BOATSWAIN

When Byron's favourite dog, Boatswain, died at Newstead the 21-year-old Byron put up a monument for him, which is still standing, and decreed that he himself was to be buried beside the dog, and old Joe Murray with him. He loved animals all his life and travelled with a menagerie including at one time three geese. He was kind to his animals and invented a special feed for his horses—bran mash with honey.

Reproduced by kind permission of Newstead Abbey, Nottingham Museums.

# NEWSTEAD ABBEY, NOTTINGHAMSHIRE

Newstead is 12 miles north of Nottingham on the A60 to Mansfield. Admission. Good Friday to September 30th, daily, 2 p.m. to 6 p.m. including Sundays and Bank Holidays. Last admission to the house at 5.15 p.m. Tours out of season by arrangement. Grounds open all year round. Tel. (0623) 793557.

The White Lady Restaurant in the south west wing is licensed. Snacks and teas in the Buttery. Open all year round. Tel (0623) 797392.

In the house is the important Roe collection of the poet's manuscripts, letters and first editions, several portraits, drawings and watercolours and his personal possessions. A huge Pilgrim's Oak stands at the entrance to Newstead on the A60. This is surprising because the Fifth Baron, who was known as the Wicked Lord, cut down and sold all the other trees on the estate to spite his son. He also slaughtered 2,000 head of deer. When the 10 year old Sixth Baron arrived from Aberdeen the mansion and grounds were almost derelict. Cattle were housed in the crypt and hay stored in the refectory. Soon after his arrival the boy planted an oak tree and its stump still stands on the south lawn.

Both house and gardens have been extensively restored since Byron's day. Mrs Byron bought seeds and set a man to work but it was a herculean task—the grounds were overgrown with weeds.

When Byron moved into Newstead at the age of 21 he chose the room next to the Prior's oratory for his bedroom. The four poster in the room today is the bed he used at Cambridge. The cover and curtains are copies of the originals. Visitors may buy the same materials. Byron got further into debt by choosing the latest thing in furnishings. This extravagance and his gambling must have led poor Mrs Byron to fear that she had another John Byron on her hands. He became more sensible and gave up gambling before he left Cambridge but when he went abroad she found he had omitted to repair the roof over all this grandeur. She had to have fires lighted constantly to prevent mildew.

In 1814 he took his half sister, Augusta Leigh to Newstead and they were snowed up together there for some weeks. Soon after this he wrote the poem which forms part of the evidence for the theory that he committed incest with his half sister:

*I speak not, I trace not, I breathe not, thy name . . .*

He left England after the separation from his wife, without ever having taken her to Newstead. He told Francis Hodgson that if he had taken her there she would have become attached to the place. He knew he must sell in order to make proper marriage settlements.

Lady Byron had behaved implacably and it is extraordinary that she went to Newstead on her own.

Lady Byron's Journal, May 22, 1818
Just come from Newstead . . .I entered the Hall—and saw the dog; then walked on into the dining room . . . he was wont to exercise there. His fencing sword and singlesticks . . . the apartments were in every respect the same . . . he might have walked in . . . the parapets and steps where he sat . . . the leads where he walked . . . his room where I was rooted having involuntarily returned . . .

Some years later Washington Irving talked to Nanny Smith who shared dominion over the servants' Hall with Old Joe Murray. Joe was butler to the old Lord and had known Byron from the age of 10. Byron loved him dearly.

'Nanny Smith was fond of Byron—A sad tale for the poor youth he being so lame. A great part of his time he spent lying on the sofa reading. Sometimes they played some mad pranks but nothing but what young gentlemen do and no harm done. Once it is true he had with him a beautiful boy as page which the housemaids said was a girl. For my part I know nothing about it. Poor soul! He was so lame he could not go out much with the men. All the comfort he had was to be a little with the ladies.'

Byron was beloved by all his servants many of whom stayed with him all his life. He was still a young man when he wrote a fatherly letter to a young servant, Robert Rushton: *I wish you to attend to your arithmetic and to occupy yourself in surveying, measuring and making yourself acquainted with every particular relative to the land of Newstead; and you will write to me one letter every week that I may know how you go on.*

---

## ANNESLEY HALL, NOTTINGHAMSHIRE

Annesley Hall, home of Byron's 'Morning Star of Annesley', Mary Chaworth, is not open to the public but can easily be seen from the roadside. From Newstead follow the drive past the Abbey and on

## OLD JOE MURRAY

Byron loved his old butler, Joe Murray, and was amused by his foibles. Joe would get up early and go out half dressed in midwinter to cut logs. 'Lord, sir', he would say, 'It's my air bath. I'm all the better for it.' Joe used to annoy Nanny Smith by singing licentious songs by the evening fire. When she heard him sing them in front of a young housemaid she read him a lecture that made his ears ring and flounced off to bed.

Produced by kind permission of Newstead Abbey, Nottingham Museums.

MARY CHAWORTH

At the age of 15 Byron fell madly in love with Mary Chaworth but she was already interested in a handsome young fox hunting squire, Jack Musters, who was more attractive than the shy, lame, overweight schoolboy. Later, when he was slim and handsome and famous she regretted her choice.

Reproduced by kind permission of Newstead Abbey, Nottingham Museums.

through the way, lined with oak trees, known as the Bridal Path. Then wind through two colliery yards and on to the A611. Head north towards the A608. You can park on the left side and see the Hall across the fields on the left. Another view can be had by turning left into the A608. The hall is on your left with the ruined church beside it.

The Wicked Lord had shot dead Mary's grandfather in a duel. Byron thought of the two families as the Montagues and Capulets. As a shy schoolboy he fell desperately in love but Mary was already interested in a handsome young fox-hunting squire called Jack Musters.

Washington Irving talked to Mary's old Nanny. She said she liked Byron.

'Ah, bless him, that I do! He used to ride over here and stay three days at a time and sleep in the blue room. Ah, poor fellow, he was very much taken with my young mistress. He used to walk about the terrace and gardens with her and seemed to love the very ground she trod on. Ah, sir, and why should I not like him? He was always main good to me when he came over. Well, well, they say it is a pity he and my young lady did not make a match of it but it was not to be. He went away to school and then Mr Musters saw her and so things took their course.'

---

## HUCKNALL, NOTTINGHAMSHIRE

From Annesley Hall take the A611 south and turn left into the B6011. The Church of St Mary Magdalen is in the village centre. In front of it is a large car park.

The Church was built in the 11th century by Sir Ralph de Burun, Byron's ancestor. Until the collieries were built the church tower could be seen from Newstead.

When Byron's body was brought home from Greece only three carriages of mourners accompanied it to Nottingham. Forty-three empty carriages escorted it to the edge of the City of London and then turned back.

The body lay overnight at the Blackamoor's Head in Nottingham and was then brought to this church. Huge crowds accompanied it and here it was laid in the family vault.

Byron's daughter, Ada, was brought up to know nothing of her

ANNESLEY HALL

Byron used to ride over from Newstead to visit Mary Chaworth here. Annesley was an orderly household, its approach decorated with pots of flowers, its gardens and terraces beautifully kept. Byron must have found it a great contrast with his own decaying mansion.

Reproduced by kind permission of Newstead Abbey, Nottingham Museums.

father but she visited Newstead as a young married woman and then decided to be buried beside her father. Her coffin lies beside his underneath the chancel.

## NOTTINGHAM

### NOTTINGHAM CASTLE AND MUSEUM, CASTLE ROAD

Admission. April to September, daily 10 a.m. to 5.45 p.m. October to March daily, 10 a.m. to 4.45 p.m. Closed Christmas Day. Tel. (0602) 411881.

Byron lived near the castle for a short time as a small boy. It was built in the 17th Century by the Dukes of Newcastle on the site of the mediaeval royal castle.

The History Gallery shows views of Nottingham as it was when Byron lived there, as well as a section on the frame shops.

The first floor Gallery possesses an oil painting by Ford Maddox Brown which has been identified as *The Chamois Hunter* from *Manfred.* If the painting is not on display, arrangements can be made to see it. A bust of Byron by A. Drury, A.R.A., stands outside the entrance.

### BREWHOUSE YARD MUSEUM, CASTLE BOULEVARD

This Museum is just below the Castle on the site of the Yard where the watermills, dovecote and Brewhouse for the Castle were. It is in a block of five 17th century houses which would have been a familiar sight to the young Byron.

Admission. All year round, daily, 10 a.m. to 12 a.m. and 1 p.m. to 5 p.m. Closed Christmas Day. Tel. (0602) 411881.

Here you may see an exhibition of placards and posters relating to the unrest in Nottingham at the time of the Luddite Riots. There are period rooms showing daily life in Nottingham.

### 76 JAMES STREET

Byron lived here with his mother for a time when they first came to Nottinghamshire. It is not open to the public. During this period Byron was tutored by Dummer Rogers who was horrified to see what pain was caused him by the contraption used by the Quack, Mr Lavender to cure the deformity of his right foot. Lavender used to send his young patient to fetch ale for him from the marketplace.

When Byron was living at Newstead he used to ride to Nottingham to attend the theatre. Mrs Siddons and other famous actors and actresses came up from London to perform here.

THE TRIP TO JERUSALEM INN, CASTLE ROAD, NEAR THE CASTLE
This is one of the oldest Inns in the country. Byron must often have walked past it.

MUSEUM OF COSTUME AND TEXTILES
The Museum is housed in a row of Georgian houses in Castlegate near the Castle.
Admission. All year round, daily from 10 a.m. to 5 p.m. Closed Christmas Day. It shows 18th and 19th Century period rooms, costumes, dolls, accessories and underwear. Tel. (0602) 411881.

RUDDINGTON FRAMEWORK KNITTERS MUSEUM,
CHAPEL STREET, RUDDINGTON
Three miles south of Nottingham in Ruddington Village, just off the Green. Admission—Tuesdays and Thursdays, April to September, 10 a.m. to 4 p.m. By appointment, all year round. Tel. (0602) 846914.

During 1811 and 1812 there were widespread Luddite riots in Nottinghamshire. Dissatisfied workers broke up the knitting frames belonging to harsh employers. The government's reaction was repression. The county was full of army encampments, militia and Bow Street Runners. Byron did not approve of the violent action taken by the workers but he sympathised with them and wrote a poem mocking *the fools who, when asked for a remedy, sent down a rope,* and he wrote to Lord Holland, *We cannot allow mankind to be sacrificed to improvements in mechanism.*

The Museum is a unique complex of early 19th Century Framework Knitters' cottages and workshops with an exhibition of the history of frame knitting. All this is directly relevant to Byron's maiden speech in the House of Lords opposing the introduction of the death penalty for frame breaking.

THRUMPTON HALL, THRUMPTON, NOTTINGHAMSHIRE

In Thrumpton Village, seven miles south of Nottingham, just off the A453, three miles east of the M1 Exit 24. Admission by prior appointment with the Hon. Mrs George Seymour. Catering by arrangement with Mrs Seymour. Evening parties to arrive by 7.30 p.m. Tel. (0602) 830333.

The house dates from the 16th century although the main part is Jacobean .

On display is a lock of the poet's hair, his signet ring, a piece of the bed-hangings from his honeymoon and a cameo of Byron and one of Lady Byron. There are also some family portraits from the Byron family; the Fourth Lord Byron and his first wife by Kneller; his children by his third wife by Parmentier and a portrait of the wife of Admiral Sir John Byron. The poet's father, John Byron, was their son. The Admiral was known as 'Foul Weather Jack' because he always met with stormy weather. Byron wrote of his grandfather:

*He had no rest at sea, nor I on shore*

---

## SOUTHWELL, NOTTINGHAMSHIRE

Take the A617 out of Newark and fork left on the A612 which will bring you in to Southwell.

*Oh, the misery of doing nothing but making love, enemies and verse!*

### SOUTHWELL MINSTER

The Minster is perhaps the most beautiful Church in England, with its great Norman nave and late 13th Century Chapter House. Inside the Minster is the Eagle lectern which came from Newstead. When the monks were driven out of the Priory at the time of the Dissolution of the Monasteries, they threw the eagle into the pond which is now known as Eagle Pond. It was rescued and brought to Southwell.

Beside the Minster is the Bishop's Manor, built into the ruins of the old Bishop's Palace where Cardinal Wolsey spent the summer of 1530 after his downfall. Behind the Minster is the 18th Century Vicar's Court. The town has many 18th century houses. The Wheatsheaf Inn is 17th Century. No. 3 Queen Street was a theatre in Byron's day. It dates from about 1630.

### THE SARACEN'S HEAD INN

In 1646 Charles I surrendered to the Scottish Commissioners in this Inn which stands opposite the Minster. The room in which he slept is still in existence. Byron took part in amateur theatricals here and flirted with the Southwell beauties at the Assemblies.

The Inn is an hotel with Bar and Restaurant and there is a car park behind it away from the main road. Tel. (0636) 812701.

### BURGAGE MANOR

During Byron's minority Mrs Byron let Newstead and rented this pleasant Georgian house on Burgage Green. She was disappointed that Byron longed to be at Newstead and found Southwell dull. He used to ride over to Newstead and stop at the Lodge with his steward, much to his mother's annoyance. He came here during his vacations from Harrow and Cambridge from 1804 to 1806. The house is not open to the public.

At the southern end of the Green is the old village pump. People from the nearby cottages and servants from the big houses would congregate there to gossip while fetching water.

### BURGAGE HOUSE

The house where Elizabeth Pigot and her brother lived stands across the Green from the Manor, facing sideways. It is not open to the public. Elizabeth became Byron's confidante during those years of conflict with his mother.

### HILL HOUSE

This house, near Burgage Green, is the 18th century house of the Rev. John Becher who told Byron he must withdraw the first printing of his first book of verse, *Fugitive Pieces* because the *Lines To Mary* were 'too warmly drawn', and 'improper for the perusal of ladies'. Byron accordingly consigned the whole edition to the flames although it was not yet paid for. He burst out laughing when the prudish clergyman asked if he might keep his own copy of the naughty book.

## NEWARK-ON-TRENT, NOTTINGHAMSHIRE

Just off the A1 north of Grantham.

### THE CLINTON ARMS, MARKET PLACE

When the young Byron had escaped from *Mrs Byron Furiosa* at Southwell by stealing out of Burgage Manor at dead of night he wrote to Elizabeth Pigot:

*I shall pass very near you on my journey through Newark—but don't tell this to Mrs B who supposes I travel a different road—if you have any letter order it to be left at Ridge's shop—on Monday I shall change horses at Newark about 6 or 8 in the evening. If your brother would ride over I should be devilish glad to see him, he can return the same night or sup with us and go home the following morning. The King's Arms is my Inn.*

That Inn, a listed Georgian building, is still dispensing hospitality under the name Clinton Arms. Tel. (0636) 72299. It is an hotel, with Bar and Restaurant.

### HOUSE OF JOHN RIDGE, THE PRINTER

The Market Place is one of the largest cobbled squares in the country and still has its old pump and bear baiting post. The Town Hall was built in 1773. The 'shop' of John Ridge stands in a corner of the square near the great church of St Mary Magdalene. It is marked by a plaque. Here Ridge printed Byron's first book of verse *Fugitive Pieces.*

Like all writers Byron was incensed by the mistakes of the printer:

*Remember in the first line to read 'loud' the winds whistle instead of 'round' which that blockhead Ridge has inserted by mistake and makes nonsense of the whole stanza.*

### MILLGATE MUSEUM OF SOCIAL AND FOLK LIFE, 48 MILLGATE

Admission—all year round, Monday to Friday 10 a.m. to 12 a.m. and 1 p.m. to 5 p.m. April to October, Saturdays and Sundays, 1.30 p.m. to 5.30 p.m. Bank Holidays 1.30 p.m. to 5.30 p.m. Tel. (0636) 79403.

Here the actual printing press used by Ridge may be seen.

### NEWARK CASTLE, CASTLEGATE

On the A46 in the centre of Newark on the banks of the Trent. Enquiries, Millgate Museum. Tel. (0636) 79403.

Admission—Easter to 30th September, daily, 1 p.m. to 5 p.m., except Monday and Thursday. Also by appointment, October to March. Gardens open all year, daily 9 a.m. to dusk. Boat trips on the River Trent set off from the river by the Castle.

Byron's ancestor, Sir Richard Byron, held the Castle for two years for the King against the Parliament during the Civil War.

# MELBOURNE HALL, MELBOURNE, DERBYSHIRE

In the village of Melbourne, eight miles south of Derby on the Ashby de la Zouch road, the A514.
Admission—Wednesdays only, 3rd June to 7th October from 2 p.m. to 6 p.m. Gardens open April to September, Wednesdays, Saturdays, Sundays, Bank Holiday Mondays. Pre-booked parties for the house by arrangement. Tel. (03316) 2502 or 3347. There is a tea room in the Stable Buildings. The formal gardens are laid out in the style of Lenotre by Henry Wise. There is a yew tunnel, a pergola, fountains, walled fruit gardens, and a lake.

Melbourne Hall belonged to the Lamb family in Byron's day. At one time George Lamb lived there and the Library is largely his. The house now belongs to the Marquis of Lothian, having descended through Lady Melbourne's daughter, Lady Emily Cowper. Among the portraits on show is the Hoppner portrait of Lady Melbourne, which hangs in the Entrance Hall.

In the Drawing Room is a firescreen said to have been worked by Lady Caroline Lamb. One of the bedrooms is associated with her husband, William Lamb, who became Queen Victoria's Prime Minster as Lord Melbourne. In a corner stands a round library table he used and above it hangs his portrait. Behind the door is a mezzotint of Lady Caroline which seems admirably to capture her strange charm.

An interesting book is on display in the Library: Madame de Staël's *Lettres sur les Ecrits et le Caractère de J. J. Rousseau par Mme La Baronne de Staël Holstein, Paris 1814.*

It is signed *'A la Duchesse de Devonshire de la part de l'auteur.'*

The Duchess in question was Lady Elizabeth Foster who had lived for many years in a sort of ménage a trois with the famous Georgiana Duchess of Devonshire, sister of Caroline Lamb's mother, Lady Bessborough, and wife of the Fifth Duke. Caroline St Jules, natural daughter of Lady Elizabeth and the Duke, married George Lamb. The book may have found its way to Melbourne Hall through her. It was probably circulated among the ladies at Melbourne House. Lady Caroline Lamb once wrote to her mother of an earlier book by Mme de Staël: 'I delight in Staël's book. It seems to me a vast fund of erudition come together God knows why but full of point and ability.'

After the death of his first Duchess the Fifth Duke married Lady Elizabeth Foster. After the Duke's death she lived for a time at what is now No. 138 Piccadilly and rented No. 139 to Byron in 1815.

## MATLOCK BATH, DERBYSHIRE

Matlock Bath is set in magnificent country in a deep gorge surrounded by high cliffs  Cable cars take visitors up to the Heights above the town.

*There are things in Derbyshire as noble as anything in Greece or Switzerland.*

Byron was 15 when Mary Chaworth's mother invited him to join a party of young people for a visit to the Spa. The outing was not wholly successful from Byron's point of view for Mary took great pleasure in dancing at an Assembly at the Old Bath Hotel and Byron leaned sulkily against the wall watching the dancing he was too lame to join.

THE TEMPLE HOTEL, TEMPLE WALK, MATLOCK BATH
Tel. (0629) 3911

The hotel is thought to have been an annexe of the original Old Bath Hotel which no longer exists. It was used for the accommodation of people of superior standing who found the Old Bath too noisy and common. It has been much altered and extended since then. An unfinished poem scratched on a window pane was thought to have been by Byron but it is dated 1786, two years before his birth.

---

## CHATSWORTH, BAKEWELL, DERBYSHIRE

In parkland on the B6012 off the A619 and the A64, four miles east of Bakewell and ten miles west of Chesterfield.
Admission—Daily, 1st April to 1st November. House—11.30 a.m. to 4.30 p.m. Garden—11.30 a.m. to 5 p.m. Pre-booked guided tours mid-week at 11 a.m. only. Tel. (024 688) 2204. Home-made hot meals and salads in the licensed restaurant in the Stable Building.

Devonshire House has gone but at Chatsworth one can view the sheer grandeur in which the Devonshire House set of Byron's time spent their lives. This set included Lady Caroline Lamb whose mother, Lady Bessborough, was the sister of the famous Georgiana, Duchess of Devonshire. Caroline's cousin, Lord Hartington, was in love with her. Years later, when he had become Sixth Duke of Devonshire, she wrote him a sad letter asking advice about what to do with Byron's letters.

In the private apartments are the Phillips portrait of Caroline Lamb and the Thorwaldsen bust of Byron. They are not normally on display but will be shown for the whole of 1988 in the great Dining Room, near the end of the regular tour of the house.

---

## PEAK CAVERN, CASTLETON, DERBYSHIRE

Just west of Castleton Village on the A625. Castleton lies at the head of the Hope Valley beneath Mam Tor, the shivering mountain. On the hill above the Cavern is Peveril Castle. Admission—daily, 11th April to 13th September, 10 a.m. to 5 p.m. Tel. (0433) 20285.

Peak Cavern is the largest natural cavern in the Peak District. There are rope walks 400 years old in the entrance. The rope-makers' cottages once formed a small village under the roof which is blackened by the smoke from their fires.

Mary Chaworth's party travelled north from Matlock Bath to Castleton. While exploring the cavern Mary and Byron had to cross an underground stream by boat, lying down together to avoid an overhanging rock. Byron wrote of the episode:

*I recollect my sensations but I cannot describe them.*

---

## CAMBRIDGE, CAMBRIDGESHIRE

*This place is wretched enough, a villainous Chaos of Dice and Drunkenness, nothing but Hazard and Burgundy, Hunting, Mathematics and Newmarket, Riot and Racing.*

Oxford and Cambridge were going through a bad patch. Fifty years earlier Gibbon had written that the Fellows had given up not only teaching but reading and thinking and their conversation consisted of Tory politics, college business, personal anecdote and private scandal.

### TRINITY COLLEGE, TRINITY STREET

Admission—Sometimes the College is closed to visitors and certain parts are open at unspecified times. The best plan is to ask at the Porter's Lodge.

Byron's rooms were thought to have been in one of the turrets in Great Court but Dr Theodore Redpath believes they were in Nevile's Court, Staircase I, 1. Byron's statue by Thorwaldsen stands at the

30

PEAK CAVERN

The mouth of the cavern is 100 feet wide and 50 feet high. Byron
and Mary Chaworth explored it together.
Reproduced by permission of the Mansell Collection.

## HON AUGUSTA LEIGH BY GEORGE HAYTER

Byron wrote of his half sister, Augusta Leigh, 'There is not a more angelic creature on earth'. She was neglected by her spendthrift husband who spent his time at the Races. Byron helped her and her children with money and fell passionately in love with her. She was a lively and charming woman who had been brought up in great houses but she was easy going and maternal and could always tease Byron out of his gloomy or dramatic moods. They first met when already grown up.

far end of the Wren Library. In the Dining Hall a small portrait of Byron hangs on the left hand wall while the Holbein Henry VIII presides over the High Table. John Edelston, the inspiration of the *Thyrza* poems, was a chorister in Trinity Chapel.

The story of the tame bear is true. Byron brought it in to annoy the Dons who had refused to allow him to have his dogs in College. There was nothing in the Statutes about bears. Byron told them it was to sit for a Fellowship. He took it back to Newstead and left it in charge of his mother when he went on his travels.

### GREAT ST MARY'S UNIVERSITY CHURCH, KING'S PARADE

An odd little scene happened here. (Noblemen who were members of the University wore splendid robes in those days.)

*Got up in the window to hear the Oratorio at St Mary's, popped down in the middle of the Messiah, tore a woeful rent in the back of my best silk gown, and damaged an egregious pair of breeches—mem. never tumble down from a church window during a service.*

### THE SENATE HOUSE, SENATE HOUSE PASSAGE, TRINITY STREET

No admission except for occasional concerts. Apply Tourist Information Centre. Tel. (0223) 322640.

On 22nd November, 1814, Byron and Hodgson, as senior members, went to the Senate House with George Lamb to vote for William Clarke in the election for a Medical Fellowship. The assembled undergraduates spotted Byron in the congregation and came to their feet to give him a standing ovation. He was surprised, embarrassed, but very moved. Their man did not win, but in 1817 he went one better and became Professor of Anatomy at Cambridge.

### ST BENE'T'S CHURCH, BENE'T STREET

Inside is a tablet to the memory of Charles Skinner Matthews, Byron's friend, who was drowned bathing in the Cam, at the fork above the Mills.

### THE EAGLE, BENE'T STREET

Dates partly from the 16th century and is partly galleried. Byron may well have sent here for ale. A pub, not a hotel.

### BYRON'S POOL

Take the Trumpington Road out of Cambridge and turn right for Grantchester. A footpath to the left leads to Byron's Pool (Sheet 45, Grid Ref: 55/43).

Byron used to ride out here with his friend, Long. A verse from Rupert Brooke refers to Byron's Pool:

'Still in the dawnlit waters cool
'His ghostly Lordship' swims his pool,
And tries the strokes, essays the tricks,
Long learned on Hellespont or Styx'

The last two rhymes are symptomatic of disapproval of 'his ghostly Lordship'.

### SWYNFORD PADDOCKS HOTEL, SIX MILE BOTTOM

This is the house that belonged to Augusta Leigh and her husband but it is much altered and extended. If you drive through Newmarket in the London direction you will find the sign for Six Mile Bottom at the roundabout near the Race Course. Tel. (063 870) 234.

Lady Frances Shelley met Byron there and related of him:

'He is decidedly handsome and can be very agreeable. He seems to be easily put out by trifles and at times looks very savage. He was very patient with Mrs Leigh's children who are not in the least in awe of him. He bore their distracting intrusions into his room (where he was writing 'The Corsair') with imperturbable good humour. Mrs Leigh has evidently great moral influence over her brother, who listens to her occasional admonitions with a sort of playful acquiescence.'

# BRIGHTON, SUSSEX

### ROYAL PAVILION, OLD STEINE

Admission—All the year round, daily, 10 a.m. to 5 p.m. June to September, 10 a.m. to 6.30 p.m. Closed Christmas Day and Boxing Day. Guided tours by appointment. Tel. (0273) 603005.

The Pavilion is undergoing extensive renovation. Parts of the upper floors may be closed.

The interior is decorated in the Chinese style. Many pieces of the original furniture are on loan from the Queen. In July, August and September, a Regency Exhibition is held and period gold, silver and porcelain is on display.

Byron visited Brighton in 1808 when he was 20 and up at

Cambridge. His companions were Gentleman Jackson, the retired prize fighter and a beautiful young girl dressed as a boy who claimed to be Byron's brother. The Pavilion Byron saw then was the original classical design of Henry Holland. The Prince Regent then decided to transform his lovely little pavilion into an Oriental Fantasy, at enormous expense. The result is a strange, magical, seaside palace. Byron may have visited the Pavilion in the summer of 1808 for he wrote to Augusta Leigh that he had seen her husband in Brighton that July. At that time Colonel Leigh was a member of the Prince Regent's Household.

BRIGHTON MUSEUM AND ART GALLERY, CHURCH STREET
Admission—All the year round, Tuesday to Saturday, 10 a.m. to 5 p.m. Sunday, 2 p.m. to 5 p.m. Closed on Mondays. Tel. (0273) 603005.

Here you can see porcelain and pottery of Byron's period; tobacco jars, flasks, furniture; a splendid library table designed by Sir John Soane for Stowe House in 1805; gilded French furniture designed for a step-uncle of Napoleon; a full sized coach and models of dress coaches, mail coaches and curricles; the full length portrait of George IV in Coronation robes by Lawrence; an evocative portrait of Lady Melbourne's daughters, Emily and Harriet as children; several portraits and objects lamenting the early death of the Princess Charlotte of Wales.

One room is devoted to models of Brighton as it was in Regency days and of the new Pavilion and its predecessor. One of the most interesting exhibits is a book:

A Dissertation on the Uses of Sea Water
In the Treatment of Diseases of the Glands
        Especially
The Scurvy, Jaundice, King's Evil, Leprosy and
The Glandular Consumption.

Translated from the Latin of Richard Russell MD
By an eminent Physician.

Dr Russel's theories may have influenced Byron to construct his cold plunge bath at Newstead.

In the same room is a display of objects connected with the fashionable craze for sea bathing.

Byron writes that he, Scrope Davies, Hobhouse and a Major Cooper *were at Brighthelmstone in the year 1808 and did in the middle of the night proceed to a house of gambling being amongst us possessed of about 20 guineas in cash . . . and we lost them. Returning home in a bad humour Cooper went home—Scrope, Hobhouse and I (it being high summer) did firstly plunge into the sea—whence after half an hour's swimming we emerged in our dressing gowns to discuss a bottle or two of champagne or hock at our quarters.*

### THE OLD SHIP HOTEL, KING'S ROAD

An Old Ship Hotel existed in Byron's day on the site of the present one. It is likely that Byron drank tea and played cards in the elegant Assembly Rooms belonging to the hotel which are in Ship Street and are still in use today. Mrs Fitzherbert used to preside over parties and balls in the Adam-style Ballroom with its Musicians Gallery.

### THE THEATRE ROYAL, NEW ROAD
#### Tel. (0273) 28488

The facade of the theatre has been altered since Byron's day but it is the same theatre which opened on 6th June, 1807, with Charles Kemble playing Hamlet and which is still showing plays, opera and ballet. In Regency days the Colonnade ran right along New Road and round the corner to allow chairmen to set down their passengers in its shelter. The theatre still has one of the prettiest painted interiors imaginable.

### THE COLONNADE BAR

Such a Bar existed in the early days of the theatre and it was said to be frequented by ladies of easy virtue. It is not unlikely that Byron and his friends foregathered there after the theatre as playgoers still do.

---

# BOWOOD HOUSE, CALNE, WILTSHIRE

Admission—Daily from either Good Friday or the 1st April until 11th October, from 11 a.m. to 6 p.m. Tel. (0249) 812102.
Entrance off the A4 in Derry Hill Village midway between Calne and Chippenham. The licensed restaurant which is very bright and pleasant, serves home produced, home cooked, lunches and teas. There is also a garden tearoom.

After the Regent had become King Byron wrote of his extravagant
work on the Pavilion

                    . . . Oh Wilberforce!
You have freed the blacks, now, pray, shut up the Whites . . .
Shut up—no, not the King, but the Pavilion,
Or else 'twill cost us all another million.
  Reproduced by kind permission of the Royal Pavilion, Art Gallery
and Museum, Brighton.

## EYWOOD HOUSE

Eywood House was the country mansion of the Earl of Oxford.
When Byron first visited his Enchantress, Lady Oxford, there, Lord
Oxford was tactfully walking about the pleasure grounds.

Bowood was one of the great Whig houses of Byron's day. The house to be seen today is a beautiful classical structure which formed part of the house Lord Holland used to visit. The pleasure grounds were designed by Capability Brown and cover 1200 acres with lake and Doric temple.

Among the paintings, drawings and sculpture on display is an Albanian costume in which Byron posed for the portrait at the National Portrait Gallery. He gave the costume to Miss Mercer Elphinstone with whom he had a brief flirtation. He admired her courage and independence for being the only one among the ladies at the famous ball given by Lady Jersey during the Separation Crisis who dared to greet him. All the other ladies left the room when he appeared and Mrs George Lamb cut Augusta Leigh dead. Miss Elphinstone married the Comte de Flahaut and their daughter married the Fourth Marquess of Lansdowne.

## BATH, SOMERSET

Bath is a splendid example of an 18th Century town.

### UPPER ASSEMBLY ROOMS, BENNET STREET

Admission— Monday to Saturday 9.30 a.m. to 5.30 p.m. Sunday 10 a.m. to 4 p.m. Closed Christmas Day and Boxing Day.

The Rooms were built in 1771 and consist of a ballroom, tea room and card room. They are still used for much the same purpose: tea dances and receptions. Here in these splendid surroundings with their magnificent chandeliers and Ionic colonnades, Catherine Gordon of Gight was dazzled by the charming manners and the elegant dancing of Captain John Byron during her fateful Bath season in 1775.

### BATH MUSEUM OF COSTUME

In the basement of the Assembly Rooms. Tel. (0225) 61111.

The costumes are displayed in period rooms and settings. Those covering 1790 to 1800, 1800 to 1810, and 1810 to 1820, show the sort of fashionable clothes worn by Byron and his mother and their contemporaries. The grey dress and pelisse worn by Annabella Milbanke for her wedding at Seaham Hall have been lent to the Museum and will be on display temporarily.

A notice in *The Bath Chronicle* announces the arrival of Mrs Byron in Bath on 28th October, 1802. A further notice tells of the arrival of the young Lord Byron on the 8th December. Mrs Byron had taken lodgings in Bath and sent for her son to spend his Christmas Holidays there. She must have taken him to see all the sights of Bath: the Abbey, the grand Pump Room, the Roman Baths. She would certainly point out to him the monument she had put up in Bath Abbey to the memory of her father, George Gordon, who had drowned himself in the Bath Canal. They may have attended services in St Michael's Church on the corner of Walcot Street and Broad Street, where she and John Byron were married.

Byron was 14 years old, quite grown up enough to be taken to assemblies at the Upper Assembly Rooms, for *The Bath Chronicle* reports that Lord Byron accompanied Mrs Byron to a Fancy Dress Ball given by a Lady Riddle who lived at No. 14 Royal Crescent.

## CHELTENHAM, GLOUCESTERSHIRE

Cheltenham was a quiet village until the second half of the 18th century. It became a Spa, George III took his family there, and soon the fashionables were going there regularly to take the waters, stroll along the parades and go to the Races. When Byron was a small boy his mother took him there. The distant view of the Malvern Hills reminded him of the mountains of Deeside.

*I can never forget the effect a few years later in England of . . . the Malvern Hills. After I returned to Cheltenham I used to watch them every evening with a sensation I cannot describe.*

In 1812 Byron wrote to Lord Holland, who was at Bowood, *By the waters of Cheltenham I sat down and drank . . . the waters have disordered me to my heart's content, you were right as you always are.*

Byron stayed at the Plough on the High Street. Caroline Lamb had been packed off to Ireland and his valet, Fletcher (who had travelled to Greece and Albania with him and who stayed with him all his life), was eager to solve his master's financial problems by marrying him off to a Dutch widow *of great riches and rotundity.* Byron was a little enamoured of an Italian Opera singer, *'Only I wish she would not swallow so much supper—chicken wings, sweetbreads, custards, peaches and port wine. A woman should never be seen eating or drinking unless it be lobster salad and champagne. I recollect asking one lady not to eat more than one fowl at a sitting, without effect.*

During this time Lady Oxford was at Georgiana Cottage on the Bath Road. Byron soon followed her home to Eywood.

Much of pre-1820 Cheltenham has been demolished over the years, including the Plough Inn and Georgiana Cottage but the Royal Crescent of today, a few minutes away from the Museum in Clarence Street, was begun in 1805 and was the fashionable place to stay by 1812. Nearby is St George's Place with several surviving late 18th and early 19th century houses.

CHELTENHAM ART GALLERY AND MUSEUM, CLARENCE STREET

Admission—All year round, Monday to Saturday, 10 a.m. to 5.30 p.m. Closed Bank Holidays. Tel. (0242) 237431).

The galleries on Cheltenham's history have on display an oil painting by J. C. Maggs showing horses being changed at the Plough Inn. This shows the early 19th century facade which may post-date Byron's visit. Another oil painting of the Inn, circa 1740, shows the timber framed houses of the High Street at that time. An aquatint by Thomas Hulley (published 1813) shows the exterior of the Assembly Rooms. Another shows the Royal Crescent. A pen and ink drawing by J. C. Nattes shows Cheltenham High Street in 1804.

PITTVILLE PUMP ROOM MUSEUM, PITTVILLE PARK

Admission—April to October, Tuesday to Sunday, 10.30 a.m. to 5 p.m. Closed Good Friday. Open Easter Monday, Spring and Autumn Bank Holidays. November to March, Tuesday to Saturday, 10.30 a.m. to 5 p.m. Closed all Winter Bank Holidays.

The museum has displays of costume from 1760 onwards including the Regency period and also a large collection of accessories, notably jewellery, many of which are Regency.

---

## THE REMAINS OF EYWOOD, Nr KINGTON, HEREFORDSHIRE

Take the B4355 north from Kington to the village of Titley. The old drive to Eywood leads off to the left in the centre of the village. The ruin is marked (Sheet 148, Grid Ref: 32/59).

Eywood was the fine Queen Anne mansion of the Earls of Oxford. Byron spent three-quarters of a year in the toils of Lady Oxford who he often referred to as the Enchantress. She was very beautiful and was married at an early age to a dull unattractive older man. She had several lovers, among them the Radical, Sir Francis Burdett. At Eywood, Byron was surrounded by books, and music, wit and humour, and much talk of politics. Lady Oxford had a horde of beautiful children of uncertain paternity and Byron spent much of his time—

*on the water, scrambling and splashing about with the children or by myself.*

(A beautiful portrait of Lady Oxford by Hoppner is owned by the Tate Gallery but is not always on display.)

All that remains of Eywood is the stable block and portico. The house was put up for sale in 1954 and in the Estate Agent's blurb occur the ominous words, 'It should be noted that the structure contains valuable quantities of fine oak and other panelling, oak flooring, mahogany doors'. The house was sold for £5,400 and demolished forthwith. The catalogue lists 'Lord Byron's bedroom (Lot 1); cornice poles and rings, sash windows, switch and four lamp holders, veined marble mantlepiece, floorboards and joists and painted panelled door with antique brass finger plates'.

The gardens, which were laid out by Capability Brown, are now overgrown—25 acres of pleasure grounds with artificial lakes. Because the road from Kington to Presteigne ran through the middle of Brown's plan, the road was diverted to preserve the privacy of the Harley family.

### KINSHAM COURT, KINSHAM

Kinsham Court is not open to the public as it is in private hands. It was the Dower House of Eywood and is 1½ miles north east of Combe, which lies on the Leominster to Presteigne road, the B4326. It may be seen from a vantage point on a hill, a little way up the lane leading from Kingsham Village to Byton.

In the grounds is a cedar known as Byron's tree because he is said to have written poetry in its shade. At the time he was working on *The Giaour* He rented Kinsham Court for a very short time and was there at times during the early part of 1813.

## KINSHAM CHURCH
(Sheet 148, Grid Ref: 36/65)

*My Kinsham premises are close to a churchyard with the most facetious epitaphs I ever read*

### A ROMAN ENCAMPMENT

While at Eywood, Byron went with Lady Oxford and her children to visit a 'Roman Encampment'. There he was accidentally hit by a stone and was a little stunned. He wrote to Lady Melbourne—

*Thank my good genius that I have still two eyes left to admire you.*

Mr Robert Jenkins of Arrow Books, Kington, tells me that the encampment was probably the Iron Age Fort on Wapley Hill which would have been described as a Roman Fort in Byron's day. It lies between Eywood and Kinsham. (Sheet 148, Grid Ref: 35/62).

Wapley Hill is a fine example of early earthwork fortification. Tradition has it that this was the last refuge of Caractacus before his final defeat by the Romans. One may be misled by the Roman Fort marked (Sheet 148, Grid Ref: 26/60) but it seems that this one was not discovered until 1965. (Mr Jenkins is very knowledgeable about local history and his second-hand book shop is well worth a visit.)

### HAY-ON-THE-WYE

One could easily combine a visit to Eywood with Hay-on-the-Wye for books.

---

## CASTLE HOWARD, CASTLE HOWARD, YORKSHIRE

Admission—daily from 25th March to 31st October. Grounds open at 10 a.m. House and Costume Gallery at 11.30 a.m. until 5 p.m. Tel. (0653 84) 333. A cafeteria in the West Wing serves home-made hot meals and salads in a bright room with flowers on the tables. Unlicensed. Parties may book ahead for restaurant meals which are licensed and served in different rooms depending on the size of the party.

Castle Howard was the house of Byron's guardian, the Fifth Earl of Carlisle. A Reynolds' portrait on display shows the Earl in the Robes of the Order of the Thistle. He was irritated by the tactless behaviour of Mrs Byron and behaved coldly toward his ward, omitting to introduce him when he took his seat in the House of Lords. Byron, thereupon, changed complimentary lines in his satire and wrote of the Earl's literary efforts as *the paralytic puling of Carlisle*. Later, he heard that the Earl had suffered from a nervous disease and was horrified at the coincidence. He made amends with some magnificent lines in *Childe Harold Canto III* in praise of Carlisle's youngest son who was killed at Waterloo.

The *Castle Howard Guide Book* advances as a possible reason for the Earl's dislike of the Byrons the fact that his mother, Isabella Byron, had left her second husband and was behaving in a scandalous manner with a French Baron. Isabella was the daughter of the Fourth Lord Byron by his third wife, Francis Berkeley. A lovely Gainsborough portrait of her is on display at the Castle.

The Howards were very kind to Augusta Byron. Lady Gertrude was one of her closest friends. Byron teased her about a story that her horse had taken her willy nilly straight into the stables at Castle Howard, much to the amusement of the family.

---

## SEAHAM. ON THE COAST NEAR DURHAM

*Upon this dreary coast we have nothing but county meetings and shipwrecks.*

Seaham was a fishing village. Sir Ralph and Lady Milbanke of Seaham Hall were the great ones of the neighbourhood. Annabella was their only child. Byron thought her interesting but 'a little encumbered with virtue'. He also feared that she would 'require all the cardinal virtues' in him. Having spotted this he was foolhardy to marry her. She refused him once and then tried to get him back. He finally proposed again rather half heartedly and then, after she had accepted him, found that his affairs had taken a turn for the worse and he could not arrange the marriage settlements. He suggested postponing the wedding but screams of protest went up from Seaham. One wedding cake went mouldy and had to be thrown away. At last the groom arrived with the faithful Hobhouse in tow. They were married in the Parlour at Seaham Hall on 2nd January, 1815.

### SEAHAM HALL

The Hall is still standing in the village of Seaham. It has been used for various purposes but there is a preservation order on the entrance,

SEAHAM HALL AND THE OLD CHURCH
This was Lady Byron's childhood home.

Detail from the *Tempesta* of Giorgione *(Accademia,* Venice). This face may be compared with that of the woman in the Triple Portrait at Alnwick Castle. One of them is the face Byron passionately admired. (See *Beppo.*)

Reproduced by kind permission of the *Accademia,* Venice.

staircase, and parlour guaranteeing that they will be maintained and free of access. How far this may be consistently carried out it is impossible to say.

On the opposite side of the stream is a small church, interesting in itself but also for a copy of the marriage Certificate with Byron's signature which hangs on the wall near the vestry. A notice in the porch explains how to gain access when the church is locked. At present, one applies to Seaham Hall Farm nearby in Lord Byron's Walk. The seashore where Lord Byron and Annabella walked together is 200 yards away.

---

## ALNWICK CASTLE, ALNWICK, NORTHUMBERLAND

This is a magnificent border fortess dating from the 11th Century. It stands above the river Aln on the north side of the town. Admission—2nd May to 2nd October, daily 1 p.m. to 5 p.m. Closed Saturdays unless Bank Holiday weekend. Tel. (0665) 602207.

The Fourth Duke of Northumberland bought a painting in Venice in the late 19th century which now hangs at Alnwick Castle under the title *The Triple Portrait,* thought to be by a follower of Titian. A new theory is that it is by Giorgione and is the painting of himself with his wife and son which is praised by Byron in *Beppo.* If so the face of the woman in the *Triple Portrait* was the object of Byron's passionate admiration:

> *'Tis but a portrait of his son and wife*
> *And self; but such a Woman! Love in Life! . . .*
> *The face recalls some face, as 'twere with pain,*
> *You once have seen but ne'er will see again . . .*
> *And, oh, the Loveliness! . . .*
> *Like the lost Pleiad . . .*

The *Triple Portrait* at Alnwick fits the description much better than Giorgione's *Tempesta,* now in the *Accademia* in Venice, though the face of the woman in the *Tempesta* is even more entrancing. The scholars are having great fun with the controversy. See Ian Scott Kilvert's interesting discussion of the case for the *Tempesta,* Byron

Journal 1981, Selby Whittingham for the *Triple Portrait*, Byron Journal 1986, and Professor Hilary Gatti on *Byron and Giorgione's wife*, *S.i.R. No. 23, Summer 1984*.

## FLODDEN FIELD

There is a car park near the battlefield on the minor road which runs from the A697 to Branxton village. A booklet on the battle may be bought at St Paul's Church (in Branxton village) where the King's body lay after the battle. There is an information board.

In 1513 the Scots, led by King James IV of Scotland, marched south to raid various border castles and to show their support for the French who had been invaded by Henry VIII. The night before the battle they lay at the village of Flodden and then took up a strong position on Flodden Hill. The Earl of Surrey led the English on a remarkable and foolhardy outflanking manoeuvre which brought his hastily gathered force in between the Scots and their way home to Scotland. King James should have attacked them during this dangerous manoeuvre, which entailed the fording of the River Till. He delayed too long and the Scots paid for it with the loss of their King, 12 earls, 15 clan chiefs and 9000 men. Among the slain was William Gordon, first Laird of Gight.

## BYRON IN LONDON

*And so—you want to come to London—it is a damned
place to be sure—but the only place in the world for fun*

*Last week I swam the Thames from Lambeth through the
two bridges, Westminster and Blackfrairs*

A statue of Byron can be seen in Hamilton Gardens at the
Apsley House (Hyde Park Corner) corner of Hyde Park.
He was born at Holles Street which runs north from Oxford
Street to Cavendish Square. The house was demolished to
make room for John Lewis's Store. A plaque by Barbara
Hepworth marks the place.

PICCADILLY TERRACE FROM HYDE PARK CORNER
TURNPIKE

Byron rented No. 13, now 139 Piccadilly, from the Dowager
Duchess of Devonshire, in 1815. There his daughter, Ada was born,
and there the bailiffs moved in.

Reproduced by kind permission of the Guildhall Library, City of
London.

# HARROW SCHOOL, HARROW ON THE HILL, MIDDLESEX

Tours of the school may be arranged. Tel. (01) 422 2196.

*We have played Eton and were most confoundedly beaten, however it was some comfort to me that I got 7 notches in the first innings and 11 in the second.*

The left hand wing of the present building was the 17th century building Byron knew. The right hand wing was added in the 19th Century. Byron's name is carved in three places on the panelling in the Fourth Form Room. In the old Speech Room Gallery is the 1822 portrait by W. E. West. A copy.

Harrovians still sing a song written in 1844 of which one verse goes:

'Byron lay, solemnly lay,
Dying for freedom far away.
Peel stood up on the famous floor,
Ruled the people and fed the poor.
None so narrow the range of Harrow,
Welcome poet and statesman too;
Doer and dreamer, dreamer, dreamer,
Doer and dreamer, dream and do.'

## CHURCH OF ST MARY'S, HARROW

In the South Transept is a plaque to the Rev. Henry Drury, one of the masters who taught Byron at Harrow. At the age of 13 Byron refused to be taught any longer by Henry Drury (who was the headmaster's son). He wrote to his mother:

*Had I stole his language could not have been more outrageous. What must the other boys think of me? Better let him take away my life than ruin my character. I may have been idle and I certainly ought not to talk in church but I have never done a mean thing in this school to him or anyone else.*

Later they became good friends.

In the churchyard is the Peachey tomb where Byron used to lie and gaze out over the countryside. Near the porch is a memorial tablet to Allegra, Byron's natural daughter by Claire Clairmont, who died in Italy at the age of five. Her grave remained unmarked for over 100 years because the powers-that-be feared for the morals of the Harrow boys.

# THE HOUSE OF LORDS, OLD PALACE YARD, WESTMINSTER SW1

This is not the building Byron knew. The Palace of Westminster burned down in 1834 except for the Crypt Chapel and Cloisters and Westminster Hall which dates from 1097.

Admission to the House of Lords is complicated. When the Houses of Parliament are in session members of the public are allowed into the Stranger's Gallery to listen to debates. The House of Lords sits from 2.30 most Mondays and all Tuesdays and Wednesdays; from 3 p.m. on Thursdays and occasionally from 11 a.m. on Fridays. Queue at St Stephen's Porch. For tours of the House of Lords UK residents should get in touch with a peer or a member of Parliament. Foreign tourists should approach their own Embassy in London.

For information Tel. 219 3107.

*A lethargic den of dullness and drawling.*

So said Byron at a moment when he was probably disenchanted by a long sitting.

He took his seat on 13th March, 1809, before going off on his travels. In March 1812, he made his maiden speech on the Government Bill to impose the Death Penalty on the Luddites. He delivered a rousing speech. The poverty he had seen in Nottinghamshire was a disgrace to a civilised country. *You call these men a mob. Are we aware of our obligations to a mob?* To condemn these men would require *twelve butchers for a jury and a Jeffries for a judge.*

Byron worked on the committee to amend the Bill but when it went back to the commons the amendments were thrown out. His second speech was on the disabilities of the Irish Catholics 14 years before Catholic Emancipation. He prophesied the dire effects of failure to redress the Irish wrongs.

His third speech was the presentation of a petition for the reform of Parliament 19 years before the first Reform Bill was passed.

When he went to the House to cast his vote during the Separation Scandal, he was hissed in the streets and all the Lords cut him except Lord Holland.

## 50 ALBEMARLE STREET, W.1

The house is not open to the public and can only be seen from the outside. It is a busy publishing house, headquarters of John Murray, descendant of Byron's publisher. It is the very house where Byron visited his publisher and met Sir Walter Scott. Later, in exile, he envied his literary friends who, he knew, would often be foregathering at 50 Albemarle Street without him. He wrote to Scott from Italy: *'The Gods be with your dreams'*, and to Thomas Moore, *'Remember me in your smiles and wine'*.

## ST JAMES'S STREET, SW1

*'I am the fashion. It's absurd but I can't help it.'*

### NO. 8 ST JAMES'S STREET

The house in which Byron was living when he 'awoke to find himself famous' has gone, but St James's Street is redolent of the 18th Century. Close to No. 8 is Pickering Place, a tiny courtyard where gentlemen used to fight duels because it was secluded and saved them an early morning drive into the country. No. 5 Pickering Place was a gambling hell. The shop on the corner, Messrs Berry and Rudd, Wine Merchants, still carry on their business behind their 18th Century shop front. Locks, the Hatters, at No. 6, have ledgers going back to the days when Nelson, Brummel and the Duke of Wellington came there for their hats. Hidden away in those old volumes may be the head size of their famous neighbour.

When *Childe Harold* was published the carriageway near No. 8 was soon jammed with carriages bringing invitations. Byron was pursued by women who fell in love with him on reading his poetry. Love letters, requests to judge literary competitions between young ladies, declarations of undying devotion, poured into St James's Street. Lady Falkland decided that because he had given her money when her husband's death left her destitute, he must be in love with her although they had hardly met. 'Why are you so cold to me, my adored boy?', she wrote to him.

Byron's head was not turned by all this adulation. He later wrote of the parties:

*Here are Bedfords, Jerseys, Ossulstones, Greys, Rogers. I never saw anything like it but a print for Dante's Inferno. All hating each other and talking.*

## THE CLUBS

No. 60 St James's Street is Brooks's Club, the chief Whig Club of Byron's day, founded by Charles James Fox. The rival Tory Club was Whites, still at No. 37. Boodles, at No. 28, was known as the *Savoir Faire*. The clubs went in for high play and were very exclusive. They are not open to the public. In Byron's day No. 64 was the Cocoa Tree Club, patronised by George IV when he was Prince of Wales and by Sheridan and later by Byron and his set.

St James's Street was well supplied with coffee houses and hotels. No. 63 was Fenton's Hotel and No. 88 the St James's Hotel. No. 74 was Thatched House Tavern and No. 87 the St James's Coffee House.

## ST JAMES'S PLACE

On the opposite side from No. 8 is St James's Place where Samuel Rogers used to give his breakfast parties at No. 22. He was a rich banker from Stoke Newington who had written a popular poem, *The Pleasures of Memory,* and everyone came to his dinners including Mme de Staël and Talleyrand. No. 22 no longer exists.

It was Rogers who told Lady Caroline Lamb 'You must meet the new poet', and gave her *Childe Harold* to read. During her love affair with Byron, Rogers would come home in the small hours to find her walking about his garden in her ball dress waiting to ask him to play go-between with Byron. Later, she portrayed Rogers as a yellow hyena in her novel, *Glenarvon.*

## ST JAMES'S PALACE, S.W.1

No admission for the public except to certain services in the Chapel Royal: Sunday Services at 8.30 a.m. and 11.15 a.m. from the first Sunday in October until Palm Sunday, on Good Friday, and the Choral Service on 6th January, the Feast of the Epiphany.

At the foot of St James's Street is St James's Palace. In the 'Summer of the Sovereigns', as Byron called it, when the Allied Sovereigns came to London to celebrate their victory over Napoleon, Blucher stayed at St James's Palace. The people crowded into Friary Court to get a glimpse of him. He often put in an appearance at the window to please them and Byron must often have heard the tumultuous applause with which they greeted him.

Augusta Leigh was granted apartments in St James's Palace on being made Bed-chamber Woman to the Queen. This was crucial for her as she was always short of money. She had to take care not to lose her place at Court on account of all the scandal, and in spite of all the gossip and rumours at the time Byron left the country, she never did. This seems to show that Royalty did not believe the rumours.

## BENNET STREET, S.W.1

This short street runs west from St James's Street to Arlington Street. In 1813 Byron lived at No. 4 which no longer exists. At this time he used to fence regularly with Henry Angelo who had taught him swordplay at Harrow, and spar with Gentleman Jackson who kept a boxing saloon in Bond Street. He had an old cleaning woman called Mrs Mule who, his friends said, looked like a scarecrow. When he moved to Albany he took her with him and when he married she was given a new wig and a new dress and promoted to Piccadilly Terrace. History does not relate what Lady Byron thought of her but Byron's friends asked him why he took the old woman about with him and he replied *the poor old devil was so kind to me*.

### THE BLUE POSTS INN

Near the site of No. 4 is the Blue Posts Inn where a caretaker claims to have heard ghostly limping footsteps in the night. In Byron's day an Inn stood near No. 4 and two blue posts in the forecourt advertised a fleet of sedan chairs plying for hire in Bennet Street. An original sedan chair stands inside the modern Blue Posts Inn. It is not an hotel but there is a restaurant upstairs called The Old Carving Room. Tel. 493 3350.

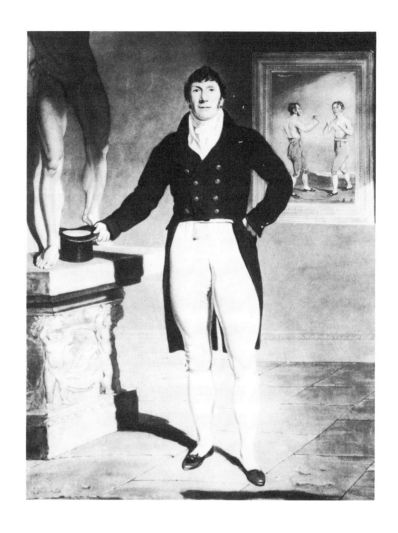

GENTLEMAN JACKSON

Byron used to spar with Andrew Jackson, the retired champion prizefighter, who had a Boxing Saloon in Bond Street.

Reproduced by kind permission of Newstead Abbey, Nottingham Museums.

# PICCADILLY, W.1

## ALBANY

Unless you know someone living there you can't go in but you can easily see the Piccadilly aspect by walking from Burlington House towards Piccadilly Circus. Albany stands set back in its own courtyard on the left. Of dark coloured brick with central porch and pediment it looks very elegant.

When the Duke of York and Albany had to sell York House it was made into exclusive Chambers for bachelors. Byron rented the set to the left of the entrance from Viscount Althorp in 1814.

*It is spacious and has room for my books and sabres*

He wrote to John Murray from Newstead:

*You will oblige me very much by making an occasional enquiry in Albany at my Chambers whether my books are kept in tolerable order and how my old woman continues in health and order as keeper of my late den.*

## 13 PICCADILLY TERRACE

After their honeymoon Byron and his bride moved in to the very grand house they could ill afford which they rented from the Duchess of Devonshire. The duns at once descended on Byron thinking mistakenly that he had come into money.

In the year of their marriage there were 10 executions in the house and the bailiffs moved in. Byron had to sell his books. He was desperately humiliated by all this. Lady Byron became pregnant almost at once. Soon after the birth of their daughter, Ada, she took the child and left him. Lady Byron refused to give any reason for leaving and the resulting scandal, fuelled by rumours put about by Byron's enemies, finally drove him out of the country. There were rumours of incest, of homosexuality, and of a crime so evil that it could not be spoken of. Byron was politically suspect and there is a theory that people in high places wanted him out of the country. Once a man became a black sheep there was no end to the vilification. (The Duke of Cumberland was accused at the same time both of murdering his valet, who was said to have found him in a compromising situation with a male servant, and of getting one of his sisters with child.) Everyone took Lady Byron's part and it is only in recent years that a less one sided view has been reached. Byron's memoirs were burned soon after his death so the full story of the marriage will never be known.

It is believed that No. 139 Piccadilly incorporates part of 13 Piccadilly Terrace but the house has been virtually rebuilt. Piccadilly Terrace faced Green Park which was then, like St James's Park, pasture land for deer and cattle. Milkmaids milked the cows and sold the milk to passers by. At the far end of Piccadilly was St James's Church. At No. 18 (early 19th century numbering) was Watier's Club, where the play was high and the food good, for it was run by the chef of the Prince Regent. Sir Walter Scott used to stay with friends at No. 15 Piccadilly West. The mailcoach for Bath set off from No. 67, the Three Coaches Inn. At No. 80 lived Sir Francis Burdett, the Radical. No. 105 was the old Deputy Ranger's Lodge of the Green Park and Lord William Gordon, brother of the Duke of Gordon, was living there when the Byrons were at No. 13. No. 160 was the house of Mr Hoby, the Bootmaker. We learn from Byron's letters that Mr Hoby was soft hearted for he wept for Queen Caroline during her trial. Hatchard, the Queen's Bookseller, was at No. 190 (now 187). Mr Hatchard used to dress like a bishop in black. People could sit by the fire in his shop and read the newspapers. The Old White Horse Cellar stood where the Ritz stands today. Nearby was Fortnum and Mason which has been there since the reign of Queen Anne. The old Pulteney Hotel was at No. 105. The Czar of Russia stayed there during the Summer of the Sovereigns and Byron must often have seen him bowing from the balcony with his sister, the Grand Duchess of Oldenburg. Not far from No. 13 was the residence of the Duke of Cambridge, now the Naval and Military Club. Farther along was Apsley House and the Hyde Park Corner Turnpike. The grandest of all the great Whig houses, Devonshire House, was where the Esso building now stands. The whole of Berkeley Square was covered by a part of its grounds. The gates of Devonshire House (wrought iron, attributed to Inigo Jones) are now at the edge of Green Park.

ROYAL ACADEMY OF ARTS, BURLINGTON HOUSE

Admission—From 10 a.m. to 6 p.m., daily, during the Summer Exhibition, which usually lasts from the first Monday in May until August. Important loan Exhibitions take place in the winter. Tel. 734 9052.

Old Burlington House was the town house of the Earls of Burlington. In the late 19th century an upper storey and grandiose wings were added. Byron wrote an account of a masked ball held there in honour of the Duke of Wellington on 1st July, 1814. Byron, dressed as a monk, tried to avoid Lady Caroline Lamb but—

LADY BYRON

Byron's memoirs were burned soon after his death so the full story of the marriage will never be known. The story we have is that told by Lady Byron with the very natural desire of justifying herself. Fletcher, Byron's valet, said, 'Every lady could manage my Lord except my Lady'.

Reproduced by kind permission of Newstead Abbey, Nottingham Museums.

## LADY CAROLINE LAMB

Byron had a brief, passionate affair with the wife of William Lamb (later Lord Melbourne), which became the great scandal of 1812-1814. After three months Byron saw that he must either run away with Lady Caroline or end the affair. He withdrew. She pursued him relentlessly until, in the end, he told Lady Melbourne, 'I must make her hate me'. She wrote, 'He broke my heart but still I love him', but she did him great harm by spreading rumours at the time of the separation from his wife.

Reproduced by kind permission of Newstead Abbey, Nottingham Museums.

*I was obliged to talk to her for she laid hold of Hobhouse and passed before where another person and myself were discussing points of Platonism so frequently and so remarkably as to make us anticipate a scene—she was masked . . . and dominoed—not all I could say could prevent her from displaying her green pantaloons every now and again though I scolded her like her grandfather upon those very uncalled for and unnecessary gesticulations.*

## THEATRE ROYAL, DRURY LANE, W.C.1
### (Tel. 836 5876)

*I never could resist the First Night of anything*

That is the remark of a true theatre lover.

Sheridan was manager of Drury Lane until 1816. It burned down and was rebuilt by 1812. Lord Holland persuaded Byron to write the address for the opening night.

In 1813 Byron used his influence to have Coleridge's play *Remorse,* put on. He knew that Coleridge was short of money and encouraged him to write more plays.

In 1815 he joined the Management Committee. He enjoyed the atmosphere of the Green Room but took his responsibilities seriously and read hundreds of plays. In a lively account of his labours he describes a—

*Mr O'Higgins, with an Irish tragedy in which the unities could not fail to be observed for the protagonist was chained by the leg to a pillar during the chief part of the performance.*

In 1815 he had a very brief affair with a young actress which he confessed to Lady Byron and she forgave him. After the separation, another actress, Mrs Mardyn, whom he had met only once, was hissed off the stage at Drury Lane because she was suspected of being Byron's mistress.

The present building has been altered but the vestibule, rotunda and skylight are original.

## ROYAL OPERA HOUSE, CONVENT GARDEN, W.C.2
### (Tel. 836 6903)

The present building opened in the late 19th century but there was an Opera House on this site in Byron's time managed by John Kemble. Byron was already a subscriber at the age of 21. He wrote from Newstead to his agent asking him to pay 40 guineas to a Lady Perceval—*the sum is for my opera subscription as I am one of her Ladyship's subscribers.*

Byron's opinion of Regency morals appears in his description of an episode at the Opera House:

*Went to my box at Covent Garden and my delicacy felt a little shocked . . . it was as if the room had been divided between your public and your understood courtesans . . . but the intrigeantes much out numbered the regular mercenaries . . . Now, where lay the difference between Pauline and her Mama and Lady \*\* and daughter except that the last two may enter Carlton and any other house and the two first are limited to the Opera and B——— house.*

#### THE KEMBLE'S HEAD
Round the corner at 60-61 Long Acre is the house where John Kemble used to live. Upstairs is a Victorian restaurant for pre-theatre dinners, whose walls are hung with plaques from performances at the Opera House. Downstairs the Pub provides bar food.

---

## HOLLAND HOUSE, HOLLAND PARK, W.8

In Kensington between Kensington High Street and Holland Park Avenue. There is a small car park.

Today, all that remains of the house is the restored east wing and the facade of the ground floor, which is used as backdrop for concerts, plays and light opera. Details are obtainable from the Park Office. Tel. 633 1707.

There is a Cafeteria open daily, February to December, from 10 a.m. until dusk. Part of the Orangery has been made into a restaurant, The Belvedere. Tel. 602 1238.

The gardens remain and one can stroll in the formal gardens laid out for Lord Holland in 1912. There he and Sydney Smith and Samuel

HOLLAND HOUSE
This was a centre of Whig politics and social life. The Hollands
became very fond of Byron.
Reproduced by permission of the Victoria and Albert Museum.

MELBOURNE HOUSE

When the Duke of York took a liking to the Melbournes' town house, now Albany, they agreed to swap it for the ducal house on Whitehall next to the Horse Guards. The rear windows looked onto St James's Park.

Reproduced by kind permission of the Guildhall Library, City of London.

Rogers listened for the nightingale, and Byron was shocked to hear Lady Holland angrily address her lame son, Henry Fox, as '*Hoppy Kicky*'.

Holland House was a great red brick Jacobean building, an easy ride into the country from the Hyde Park Corner Turnpike. In Byron's day it was the hub of the Whig party. Sheridan, Lord Grey, Sydney Smith, the Melbournes, the Bessboroughs, the Granvilles, foreign ambassadors, refugee noblemen, the wits, the painters, the scientists, all flocked to Lady Holland's dinners and hoped to be asked to stay the night. Byron had satirised the Holland House dinners in *English Bards and Scotch Reviewers* but the Hollands became very fond of him. After his death Lady Holland said 'I can still see him sitting there under that lamp looking so beautiful'. Lady Holland was a formidable woman who had been a great beauty. Sydney Smith claimed that there was a chemist in Kensington who made up special pills for people who had been frightened by Lady Holland.

## MELBOURNE HOUSE, WHITEHALL, S.W.1

Walk up Whitehall from Parliament Square past Downing Street and the Cenotaph. Melbourne House stands next to the Horse Guards and can also be seen from Horse Guards Parade. It is now the Scottish Office and is not open to visitors.

In Byron's day it was one of the great Whig mansions. Lord and Lady Melbourne lived on the ground floor. Their second son, William, and his wife, Lady Caroline, on the first floor. Here, Byron first called on Lady Caroline and, when the affair was breaking up, he called regularly on Lady Melbourne, who became his confidante, much to the disgust of the Prince Regent, who said he never heard anything like it—taking the mothers for confidantes. When the waltz was first introduced from Germany, morning parties were held at Melbourne House for practising this daring new dance. Here, Byron first caught sight of the prim and priggish Miss Annabella Milbanke who, he later wrote, *was born for my desolation*.

The Prince Regent's Carlton House was nearby in what is now Waterloo Place. Prinny could easily cross the corner of St James's Park for his candle-lit dinners alone with his hostess at Melbourne House. Lady Melbourne was said to have gained the peerage for her husband by an intrigue with the Regent.

# WESTMINSTER ABBEY, S.W.1

The entrance is from Broad Sanctuary by the west door. Admission—daily, 8 a.m. to 6 p.m. Wednesdays, 8 a.m. to 7.45 p.m. Sundays, only the nave and the nave aisles are open.

*I should prefer a grey Greek stone to Westminster Abbey*

The Greeks wanted to bury Byron in their Temple of Theseus. Westminster turned away not only his body but even his statue. It was not until more than a hundred years after his death that a memorial tablet was allowed in Poet's Corner. In the Abbey are monuments and graves of several notable contemporaries. Byron could have expected to rest among them. Henry Grattan, Wilberforce, Fox and the Younger Pitt are buried in the North Transept near statues of Castlereagh, Peel, Canning.

In Poet's Corner are the grave of Sheridan and statues of Wordsworth, and Campbell, busts of Coleridge, Southey, Burns, Garrick, Sheridan and Sir Walter Scott and plaques to Keats and Shelley. In the North Chapel are statues of Mrs Siddons and Kemble and a tablet to Sir Humphrey Davy.

Sheridan, Burns and Fox all led highly immoral and well publicised lives. The question is, why were they allowed in while Byron was debarred. I believe the answer is the extraordinary fame of Byron which magnified every failing and gave rise to the most exaggerated stories of his supposed evil-doings. In Italy the rumour was that he had shut up his wife in one of his castles (sic) for several years out of revenge. In France, the Dictionary of National Biography solemnly told its readers that Byron had murdered one of his mistresses and habitually drank wine out of her skull. A preacher in Kennington declared that, having drained the cup of sin to its dregs, he was no longer human but a cool unconcerned fiend.

Byron wrote in 1816, as he prepared to leave the country,

*I have now been compared to Nero, Apicius, Heliogabalus, Epicurus, Caligula, Henry VIII and the Devil. Were I to be beaten down by the world and its inheritors I would have succumbed long ago.*

Less than a year later he sent—

*A sigh to those who love me*
*And a smile to those who hate.*

CHURCH OF ST MARY MAGDALENE, HUCKNALL

In this church, which was built by his ancestor, Sir Ralph de Burun, in the 11th century (and has been much altered and extended), Byron's body was buried in the vault under the chancel. His mother was buried there before him and his daughter, Ada, who died at the age of 36, insisted on being laid to rest beside her father.

Reproduced by permission of the *London Illustrated News* Picture Library.

This statue by Thorwaldsen, was intended for Westminster Abbey.
It was turned away and finally went to Trinity College, Cambridge,
where it stands in the Wren Library.

Reproduced by kind permission of the Master and Fellows of
Trinity College, Cambridge.

# APPENDIX

## SOME PAINTINGS AND PRINTS OF BYRON'S PERIOD

*Anyone travelling in search of Byron would do well to start with the portraits of Byron and his contemporaries.*

### The National Portrait Gallery

St Martin's Place, WC2, near the National Gallery. Admission— Monday to Friday, 10 a.m. to 5 p.m., Saturday, 10 a.m. to 6 p.m. Sunday, 2 p.m. to 6 p.m. Closed New Year's Day, Good Friday, May Day Monday, Christmas Eve and Day and Boxing Day. Tel. 930 1552.

*The Regency Gallery, Room 14*
George IV, the Duke of Cumberland, Princess Caroline of Brunswick, Mrs Fitzherbert, the Princess Charlotte of Wales, a large painting of the Trial of Queen Caroline showing the lawyers, Lushington and Brougham (who later collaborated against Byron), the Duke of Clarence. Sir John Soane, Sydney Smith, Francis Jeffrey, Lord Liverpool, Addington, Castlereagh, Lord Grey, Sir Francis Burdett, William Cobbett, William Hone, Francis Place, Jem Belcher (the prize fighter), Mme Catalini (the singer), Henry Angelo (the fencing master), Charles Kemble (the actor), Mrs Siddons.

*The Romantics, Room 13*
Keats, Shelley, Mary Shelley, Coleridge, Clare, Wordsworth, Byron in Albanian Costume, Leigh Hunt, Southey, William Godwin, Crabbe, Sir Walter Scott, Burns.

*Britain at War, Room 12*
William Pitt the Younger, Nelson, Wellington, Paine, Burke, Sir James Macintosh, the Duke of York as C-in-C. A bust of Fox.
Some cartoons on war, one or two by Gillray.

*Regency Drawings*
In this room is the bust of Byron by Bartolini, drawings of Lady Jersey, Lord Elgin, Tom Cribb, a Staffordshire set of a fight between Cribb and Molyneux.
In the earlier rooms you may see George III as a young man and as a mad, blind, old man, Alexander Pope (Byron's most admired poet), Sheridan and Napoleon.

69

## National Gallery
Trafalgar Square, WC2.
Admission—Monday to Saturday, 10 a.m. to 6 p.m., Sunday 2 p.m.
to 6 p.m. Closed New Year's Day, Good Friday, May Day Monday,
Christmas Eve and Day. Tel. 839 3321.

*Rooms 35 to 39. The British School of Painting*
The Stubbs, the Zoffanys, the Gainsboroughs, the Reynolds, give a
picture of the wealth and elegance of the period into which Byron was
born. *The Melbourne and Milbanke Families* by Stubbs shows Lady
Melbourne as a young woman in a curricle with her husband, then Sir
Penistone Lamb, her father, and her brother, Ralph, (Lady Byron's
father). The Hogarth series, *Marriage a la Mode,* is a social
commentary on the times.

## London Museum
London Wall, EC1.
Admission—Tuesday to Saturday, 10 a.m. to 6 p.m. Closed New
Year's Day, Christmas Eve and Day and Boxing Day. Tel. 600 3699.
   Here are paintings and drawings of 18th century London—shop
fronts, tavern signs, a whipping post, a cell from a debtors prison.
The London Museum also has prints and water colours which can be
ordered for inspection from the reserve collections. Among these are
a set of watercolours by Rowlandson and a book of later reprints of
Gillray.

## Victoria & Albert Museum
Brompton Road, South Kensington, SW7.
Admission—Monday to Thursday and Saturday, 10 a.m. to 5.50 p.m.
Sunday, 1.30 p.m. to 5.50 p.m. Closed Fridays and New Year's Day,
May Day Monday, Christmas Eve and Day, and Boxing Day. Tel. 589
6371.
*In Room 40* is a display of costume, dolls and fans among which are
fashionable 18th and early 19th century clothes.
*Rooms 122 to 125* show English furniture and Decorative Arts of 1750
to 1830.
*Room 121* shows Regency furniture, silver and ceramics.
*Room 50* shows English sculpture including busts of George III and
Charles James Fox.

70

*Room 202* Prints and Drawings.

*Rooms 217 to 221* contain British paintings of the 18th and 19th centuries and also a Delacroix painting of the shipwreck in *Don Juan*.

## Sir John Soane's Museum
13 Lincoln's Inn Fields, WC2.
Admission—Tuesday to Saturday, 10 a.m. to 5 p.m., all the year round. Closed Sunday, Monday and Bank Holidays. Tel. 405 2107.

*The Picture Room*
A look at the two series of paintings by Hogarth would be a good way to find out what Byron's satirical and political poetry was all about: *The Election* and *The Rake's Progress*. Hogarth was earlier than Byron but it was not until the 1820's that serious efforts at reform were made.

## The British Museum
Great Russell Street, WC1
Admission—Monday to Saturday, 10 a.m. to 5 p.m., Sunday 2.30 p.m. to 6 p.m. Closed, New Year's Day, Good Friday, May Day Monday, Christmas Eve and Day, and Boxing Day. Tel. 636 1555.

Turn left inside the main entrance for the Elgin Marbles. Byron's *Curse of Minerva* and some stanzas from *Childe Harold* are on the subject of the removal of the sculptures from Greece. The question is fraught with difficulties.

## Scottish National Portrait Gallery
1 Queen Street, Edinburgh.
Admission—Monday to Saturday, 10 a.m. to 5 p.m. Sunday, 2 p.m. to 5 p.m. Closed Christmas Day, Boxing Day, 1st and 2nd January, and May Day. Tel. (031 556) 8921.

The portrait of Byron by West hangs in the room with portraits of Burns, Sir Walter Scott, and Hogg, and the Edinburgh Reviewers, Jeffrey and Brougham.

## THE PRINTS AND DRAWINGS OF BYRON'S PERIOD

The prints, drawings, watercolours, broadsheets, caricatures, and lampoons, which were published in the early 19th century are a commentary on the social and political background to Byron's poetry. Unfortunately, they are not as readily accessible as the paintings of Hogarth as art work on paper is extremely delicate and can be damaged by exposure to light and by careless handling. Many are stored in the print rooms of the British Museum and the Victoria and Albert Museum. The best are by Gillray, Rowlandson and Cruikshank.

*The Prints and Drawings Room at the British Museum*
Admission—Monday to Friday 10 a.m. to 1 p.m., 2.15 p.m. to 4 p.m. Saturdays 10 a.m. to 12.30 a.m.
   Application to study the collection is made by completing Form BM Students 8A which asks applicants to state their occupation and the purpose for which they request admission. A signed recommendation is required from someone not a relative, of recognised position. Applicants must be 18 years or over. Tel. 636 1555. Ask for Prints and Drawings.

*Victoria & Albert Museum, Print Room*
Admission—Monday to Thursday from 10 a.m. to 4.30 p.m. Saturday, 10 a.m. to 4.30 p.m. but closed from 1 p.m. to 2 p.m. for lunch. No ticket or application form or recommendation is required. Tel. 589 6371.

*"Where is the world?" cried Young at eighty—"Where*
*The World in which a man was born?" Alas!*
*Where is the world of eight years past? 'Twas there—*
*I look for it—'tis gone, a globe of glass!*
*Cracked, shivered, vanished, scarcely gazed on, ere*
*A silent change dissolves the glittering mass.*
*Statesmen, Chiefs, Orators, Queens, Patriots, Kings,*
*And Dandies—all are gone on the wind's wings.*

# IN SEARCH OF THE FAMOUS GUIDE BOOKS

*Projected titles*

In Search of Byron Abroad

In Search of Sir Walter Raleigh in England, Ireland and
the Americas

In Search of Richard III

sex and v.d.

# sex

# and

# v.d.

Derek Llewellyn-Jones

OBE MD MAO FRCOG

*with illustrations by Audrey Besterman*

Faber and Faber
3 Queen Square
London

*First published in 1974*
*by Faber and Faber Limited*
*3 Queen Square London WC1*
*Printed in Great Britain by*
*Butler & Tanner Ltd*
*Frome and London*

*ISBN 0 571 10482 7 (hard bound edition)*
*ISBN 0 571 10483 5 (paper covers)*

# contents

1 the problem  *p. 11*

2 female and male  *p. 23*

3 about gonorrhoea  *p. 41*

4 about syphilis  *p. 51*

5 Moses, Columbus and venereal disease  *p. 72*

6 other sexually transmitted diseases  *p. 91*

7 nine points for thought  *p. 106*

further reading  *p. 109*

index  *p. 110*

# list of illustrations

2/1  The external genitals of a virgin  *p. 26*

2/2  The external genitals of a woman who has had a
child  *p. 27*

2/3  The internal genital organs of a woman  *p. 29*

2/4  The cavity of the uterus viewed from the front  *p. 31*

2/5  The uncircumcised penis and scrotum (foreskin
retracted on the right)  *p. 34*

2/6  The erect penis showing the glans penis and the
frenulum  *p. 35*

2/7  The external and internal genital organs of a man  *p. 38*

2/8  The epididymis and testis  *p. 40*

3/1  Gonorrhoeal urethral discharge  *p. 44*

3/2  The spread of gonorrhoea  *p. 46*

3/3  The gonococcus seen through the microscope  *p. 47*

4/1  *Treponema pallidum* and pus cells seen under a
microscope  *p. 52*

4/2  The primary lesion of syphilis in a man – a chancre
on the penis  *p. 56*

4/3  The primary lesion of syphilis in a woman – a chancre
on a labium, with enlarged lymph glands in the groin  *p. 57*

4/4  The secondary rash of syphilis  *p. 59*

4/5  The secondary stage of syphilis  *p. 60*

4/6  Syphilitic warts on the vulva  *p. 61*

4/7  Mucous patches in the mouth  *p. 62*

4/8  The natural history of untreated syphilis  *p. 64*

4/9  A gumma on the leg  *p. 66*

4/10  Prenatal syphilitic infection  *p. 69*

5/1  Le Bagage, or the camp follower  *p. 77*

5/2  St. Denis supplicates the Virgin Mary to help a victim
of the new disease  *p. 81*

5/3  The decline in the incidence of syphilis since
1946  *p. 86*

5/4  The rise in the incidence of gonorrhoea in the United
Kingdom since 1955  *p. 88*

6/1  Non-specific urethritis seen through a microscope
(compare with Fig. 3/3)  *p. 92*

6/2  Trichomonads seen under a microscope  *p. 95*

6/3  *Candida albicans* seen through a microscope  *p. 101*

6/4  Chancroid  *p. 105*

*To the memory of Philippe Ricord, born in 1799,
and died in 1889, an eminent venereologist who
finally identified that gonorrhoea and syphilis
were two separate diseases, and of whom Oliver
Wendell Holmes wrote 'he was the Voltaire of
pelvic literature – a skeptic as to the mortality of
the race in general, who would have submitted
Diana to treatment with his mineral specifics and
ordered a course of blue pills for the Vestal Virgins.'*

# 1

# the problem of venereal disease today

Information obtained from many nations of the world by the World Health Organization confirms that, in the past fifteen years, the number of cases of sexually transmitted diseases has been increasing. This increase applies particularly to the three sexually transmitted diseases which constitute, in law, the venereal diseases. These are gonorrhoea, syphilis and chancroid. They obtained their name from Venus, the goddess of love. Since the organisms which cause the diseases usually enter the body during sexual intercourse with an infected person, the term was a useful one. But it has been realized, in recent years, that other diseases may be transmitted during sexual intercourse, so that the term sexually transmitted disease is more appropriate.

The World Health Organization states that gonorrhoea is the world's second most common infectious disease (only measles is more common). It was estimated in 1970 that over 200 million people were infected that year. In the same year it was estimated that syphilis had been detected in 50 million people. Accurate figures are impossible to obtain. Sample surveys in the U.S.A., Britain and Australia, to name only three countries, show that only 10 per cent of cases of gonorrhoea and only 30 to 50 per cent of cases of syphilis treated by private doctors are reported, although, in law, doctors have an obligation to make a report to the health authorities.

The obligation to report cases of gonorrhoea and syphilis is not just to obtain statistics. The two diseases are infectious and contagious. This means that they are transferred easily from an infected person to a non-infected person by contact. The only difference between the venereal diseases, and other contagious diseases, is that the contact usually occurs during sexual intercourse. In Western society, sexual intercourse is not discussed openly, and infection acquired during sexual intercourse is thought by society, and by the infected person, to be disgusting, indecent and something to be concealed. The control of any infectious disease depends on treating the infected person and in tracing infected contacts so that they may be treated. The purpose of informing the health authorities that a person has contracted gonorrhoea or syphilis is to enable them to do just this; and patients or their doctors who refuse to cooperate – as all too many do – are encouraging the spread of an easily treated disease.

Unfortunately ignorance and prejudice about venereal diseases is widespread, and many doctors are as ignorant as is the general public. Many doctors show attitudes of disapproval and condemnation when a patient, who thinks he may have a sexually transmitted disease, seeks advice. Many patients, particularly young people who are increasingly being infected, are apprehensive, fearful and ashamed to seek help, in case the doctor is critical and disapproving. Because of this they conceal the disease in the hope that the symptoms will go away. They often do, but unfortunately the individual continues to be infective.

Many myths have arisen because venereal diseases are

not discussed openly. What should be remembered is that most people who have gonorrhoea or syphilis cease to be infectious within 24 hours of starting treatment, although they must continue to attend their doctor, or the hospital clinic, until the experts are sure that they have been cured completely.

This disapproving attitude to the sexually transmitted diseases extends to the type of clinic where advice and treatment is given. All too often it is in an ugly building, difficult to find, unpleasant to attend, uncomfortable to wait in, dirty and dingy. As venereal diseases have a marked social stigma, many possible patients are reluctant to attend for treatment, and many an anxious patient is deterred when he or she sees the inadequate facilities. This reticence would be overcome to some extent, if the clinics were in well-appointed and pleasant buildings, in convenient areas, open at convenient times, where first-class treatment was given, where the patient knew he would be treated confidentially without any moral strictures being passed, and where all treatment was free.

Nothing of what I have written so far explains why there has been such a considerable upsurge in the venereal diseases in recent years. It is a strange paradox that the increase has occurred at a time when, in many nations, affluence has never been greater, education is widespread, and the treatment for sexually transmitted disease is painless and very effective.

The principal reason for the increase seems to be an increasingly 'permissive' attitude to sexuality. If no individual ever had sexual intercourse, except with the partner he, or she, had married, the diseases would almost certainly be eradicated. As this situation has never applied in the whole history of mankind (except perhaps in the mythical garden of Eden!), it is entirely unrealistic to expect it to happen now. Human sexuality is a deep and forceful drive, which most people need to overcome by masturbation, or by copulation, whatever moralists may say. It is also influenced by fashion, and when fashion adopts an increased 'permissiveness' in sexual relations, venereal diseases are likely to spread.

For several centuries, in Western nations, there has been a double standard of sexuality. Young men, if not encouraged, at least were not discouraged, or disapproved of, when they copulated. Young women were meant to remain chaste until marriage. But for young men to copulate, they had to have partners, who were usually female. Some of them had venereal disease and infected the young men, who in turn infected the chaste young women after marriage.

In recent years many young women have rejected this double standard, and have joined the ranks of those who copulate. In recent years there has been more casual copulation, and an increase in the sexual activity, by young people under the age of 20. These two factors have had a considerable effect on the incidence of the venereal diseases, and account to a large extent for the great incidence in infections found amongst teenagers.

The increased sexual activity of women has had a further effect. Women who are infected with gonorrhoea often have no symptoms, or such mild symptoms that they ignore them. But they are infectious and they may infect their next sexual partners for weeks or months or even years. In two

14

large series of patients, investigated by two eminent physicians specializing in venereal diseases, between 50 and 80 per cent of women diagnosed as having gonorrhoea were completely symptomless and only attended the hospital because they had been asked to do so by their infected sexual partner. This large 'reservoir' of women with symptomless, silent, gonorrhoea is one reason for its spread, particularly if the infected woman is sexually active with several partners. In other words, if she is promiscuous.

The spread of venereal diseases has been encouraged in Europe and the U.S.A. by the increasing mobility of people and the development of cheap package holidays. Many European countries have sought foreign-born workers to man their booming factories. These men, who are usually young and single, come from the poorer nations of Southern Europe, North Africa and West Asia. They tend to live in groups in the larger industrial cities. They are frequently bored and lonely, and find transient companionship and contact with local girls in clubs and pubs. The girls are often emotionally unstable, sexually active and infected with symptomless gonorrhoea or untreated syphilis. Britain, in the 1960s, accepted large numbers of immigrants from the Carribean, Pakistan and India. These migrants, like the migrant workers of Europe, concentrated in the larger industrial cities where there was a better chance of finding work, and where they could mix more readily with people from their homeland. Like the European migrant workers they sought companionship in pubs and clubs, and as in Europe, local girls were sexually willing, sexually able and often infected. So venereal disease spread. This led to the myth, still firmly believed by many English people, that the coloured migrants brought venereal diseases with them. The evidence is that the majority of migrants obtained their infection from local girls, and were uninfected when they arrived in Britain. This had led one British authority, Dr. Morton, to state 'My own experience is that much more infection is imported by U.K.-born tourists returning from the continent' than by immigrants.

The factor of increased travel and tourism has undoubtedly led to an increase in venereal disease. Away from home, free from the constraints of his own environment, warm with sun and alcohol, relaxed and sedated, casual copulation not only seems sensible but pleasurable and desirable to the holiday-maker. And to meet the demand, a supply of local girls is available. Many have either gonorrhoea or infective syphilis. The evidence that these casual encounters lead to an increase in venereal disease is demonstrated by figures from Sweden and Holland which show that 20 per cent of all cases of infectious syphilis diagnosed in 1965 was imported by returning tourists, or by businessmen. Yet when these people return home, they are all too ready to criticize the 'permissive' young whilst ignoring their own sexual activities.

Many students, in many nations, have shown that merchant sailors and members of the Armed Forces are particularly likely to be infected with sexually transmitted diseases and to infect others. Deprived of female company for long periods and relatively rich when they reach a port, they are particularly susceptible to advances by local prostitutes or enthusiastic amateur fornicators. The high incidence of a particularly resistant strain of gonorrhoea acquired by the U.S. servicemen in Vietnam, and passed on gratuitously to women in countries as far apart as Austria and Australia, is an example of this. Indeed, any men, or women, who

16

are itinerant, such as commercial travellers, cane cutters, pea pickers, transient workers, and particularly lorry drivers, have a higher than average risk of acquiring, and spreading, venereal disease.

A perceptive observer in Denmark, Dr. Ekstrom, has identified another group who have a high risk of acquiring a sexually transmitted disease. He remarks that venereal disease control is not only a question of diagnosis and treatment. It is also a social problem, particularly amongst teenagers, as many of those infected have a less favourable social background than the rest of the population. They have poor relationships with their parents, they often come from broken homes, they have frequent changes of schools and jobs, and, obviously, of sexual partners. They are no less intelligent than other teenagers. Dr. Ekstrom believes that additional education in the social aspects of life is needed in schools, and more importantly there is a need to improve social conditions for the at-risk group.

In several studies, homosexuality has been implicated in the spread of venereal disease. These studies refer to male homosexuals, who are claimed to be particularly promiscuous.

In an investigation in London in 1966, one doctor reported that nearly 20 per cent of all the cases of gonorrhoea he saw in this clinic, were in practising homosexual men. However, his experience may be exceptional. In Holland in 1969, only 5 per cent of infected men said that they had acquired the infection from a homosexual partner. And as between 5 and 10 per cent of men are homosexual, the promiscuity of homosexuals may be exaggerated.

A problem of the promiscuous homosexual is that he may have a symptomless gonococcal infection. In his case the

17

infection is in his anus and rectum, so that when anal sexual intercourse takes place, his partner is infected. What is not clear is whether homosexuals are sexually promiscuous because of an emotional defect, or whether their promiscuity is due to society's reaction to homosexuality and the fear many homosexuals have of being condemned, criticized and even prosecuted if they form a permanent relationship with another man.

In all nations, whether in the rich, affluent, developed third of the world, or in the hungry, developing two-thirds of the world, there is a drift to the cities. This has been going on for the past 50 years but is currently gathering momentum. One calculation suggests that by 2000 A.D., only 25 years from now, over 80 per cent of people in the developed nations, and over 55 per cent of people in the developing nations, will live in towns. Many of those migrating to escape the boredom and rigidity of village life are single, young and anxious to throw off the constraints of their old life. They are likely to seek solace, when lonely, with city girls, some of whom will certainly be infected with gonorrhoea or syphilis.

Those who have followed the argument this far will appreciate that there is no single cause for the accelerating increase in venereal disease, which has become, in the words of the World Health Organization, 'a world-wide epidemic'. The sexually transmitted diseases infect people of all classes, all professions and all races. All that is needed is to have sexual intercourse with an infectious partner. The statistics do show a startling increase in the frequency of the disease in teenagers, and especially teen-aged girls, but

18

no age is exempt. Men are twice as likely to be infected as are women, but this is merely because men copulate casually more often than women. It is true, as Dr. Catterall writes, that 'In the final analysis the problem is a moral one and depends upon the standards of sexual behaviour which prevail in the community as a whole. Promiscuity results in the spread of venereal diseases and they cannot be contracted if risks of infection are not taken.' But this statement is no help, for casual sexual intercourse is not prevented by exhortation, nor was it in the periods of history which were apparently sexually repressive.

What is needed is realism. Most people are not going to change their attitudes to their own sexuality, and many are going to continue to have casual sexual intercourse, whatever moralists say. An increasing number of people believe that sexual intercourse between consenting adults, whether hetero- or homosexual, is a personal matter and should not be interfered with by society. Society must recognize these facts, and rather than condemn silently, must attempt to reduce the dangers of promiscuity. These dangers are unwanted pregnancies and the spread of the sexually transmitted diseases.

In part, the change will come through education; in part through the change in the attitude of the opinion-makers, and the leaders of society, towards venereal disease.

Since human sexuality is such a deep, instinctive drive, knowledge of human sexuality and its consequences should form part of the education of every individual. As I have discussed in another book, *Human Reproduction and Society,* I believe that education in human sexuality, including sexual responsibility, should extend throughout the school years, starting at the age of 8 or 9. Factual knowledge about

19

the sexually transmitted diseases should have been given, and discussions held in mixed classes, before the children reach puberty. This educational experience may deter some from later casual sex, and induce those who wish to be promiscuous to seek medical help, without fear or shame, should they get a venereal disease. Whether education alone will reduce V.D. will only be found out by experience. It will not increase casual sexuality, or 'harm the fabric of society,' as certain conservatives believe. The evidence from Scandinavia is clear on this point.

As I have mentioned, the sexually transmitted diseases, particularly the major diseases, gonorrhoea and syphilis, are infectious and contagious. The spread of the diseases will only be arrested if each person with whom an infected individual has had sexual intercourse is contacted, examined and, if infected, is treated. In most Western countries, the traditional method of 'contact tracing' is for the doctor who treats the person to hand him, or her, a contact slip or slips to give to his sexual partner or partners, asking them to go to a hospital or to a private doctor, taking the slips with them. This method has not been very successful, particularly among the 90 per cent of patients who seek private treatment from a private doctor. Increasing numbers of people believe that contacts should be sought by specially trained social workers who could more readily persuade them to be examined, and if needed to be treated. This method seems to have worked in the U.S.S.R., where an efficient venereal disease service has been established. The names of all patients who have contracted venereal disease, and their known sexual partners, are compulsorily (but confidentially) notified to special health workers, who make the contacts. In the U.S.S.R., the incidence of venereal disease

20

is declining, at a time when it is rising in the other developed nations.

Whether compulsion will be needed in other nations is uncertain, but there is no reason why the public should object. They do not object to the compulsory notification of diphtheria, poliomyelitis, typhoid fever or other infectious diseases. The acceptance of compulsory notification and contact tracing by trained and carefully selected health workers would be more readily accepted, if the public's inaccurate understanding of the nature of the sexually transmitted diseases was improved by using the media to educate them in an imaginative manner.

A campaign should also be initiated using radio, television and magazines to induce high risk groups, particularly promiscuous homosexual men, and prostitutes, to seek voluntary examinations at regular intervals.

From the point of view of the individual who is at risk of catching venereal disease, what should be done? The purpose of this book is to explain just this. But in summary, any person, who after sexual intercourse is concerned that he or she has acquired a sexually transmittable disease, should visit his doctor or a hospital so that tests can be made. He should not be afraid or ashamed to make a visit.

Because so many women, infected with gonorrhoea, have no knowledge that they have the disease, any woman who has multiple sexual partners should go for examination at periodic intervals. She should neither be fearful nor ashamed, for her sexuality is her own affair and the only function of the doctor is to detect and treat a possible infection.

A question which may be asked is: what are the chances of me getting venereal disease if I have casual sexual intercourse with an infected partner? This is very difficult to de-termine, but the evidence is that nine out of every ten per-sons, whether male of female, acquire gonorrhoea if they have sexual intercourse with an infected partner. And about one in every three people who have intercourse with a partner who has active syphilis will develop syphilis. These figures apply to a single casual episode of sexual intercourse. Repeated sexual intercourse with an infected partner makes it much more likely that you will catch the diseases.

As well as these measures, medical research is urgently needed. Science has devised and produced vaccination against poliomyelitis, diphtheria, whooping-cough, rubella, measles, typhoid and smallpox, to name but a few. If funds were made available it should be possible to develop vaccines against gonorrhoea and syphilis within a short time. But funds will only be made available if the authorities, and the public, stop putting the venereal diseases in a special category, and treat them for what they are – infectious dis-eases which are spread by sexual intercourse.

It is an odd comment on society that man can spend $120 billion dollars to go to the moon and merely bring back some kilograms of rock, but mankind cannot devise a vaccine which eliminates gonorrhoea, which last year infected at least 200 million people, or syphilis, which infected 50 million. Eight years ago, speaking in Denver, Colorado, one American authority, Dr. Knox, said wryly that if as much money was put into venereal disease re-search as went into research into poliomyelitis, which neither cripples nor kills as many people, a vaccine could be found in a few years.

Nothing has been done yet. The public has a right to ask why.

# 2

# female

# and

# male

In the great majority of instances the organisms which cause the sexually transmitted diseases gain entry to the human body through the genitals. In a few cases, the organism which causes syphilis – the *Treponema pallidum* – is transferred from the mother's blood to that of the unborn baby through the afterbirth. Sometimes a woman, or a homosexual man, is infected on the tongue or the lips when sucking the infected penis of a sexual partner. Sometimes a man may be infected in a similar way by kissing an infected woman's vulval area.

The organism which causes gonorrhoea may spread from its place of entry (which is usually the urethra), particularly in women, to invade other organs which make up the genital tract. Men, too, may experience spread to the internal genital organs or to the testicles.

A knowledge of the anatomy of the genital organs is important if the sexually transmitted diseases are to be understood fully.

## woman

The anatomical name for the area of the external genitals in the female is the vulva. It is made up of several structures which surround the entrance to the vagina, and each of

23

which has its own separate function (Fig. 2/1). The labia majora (or the large lips of the vagina) are two large folds of skin which contain sweat glands and hair follicles embedded in fat. The size of the labia majora varies considerably. In infancy and in old age they are small, and the fat is not present; in the reproductive years, between puberty and the menopause, they are well filled with fatty tissue. In front (looked at from between the legs), they join together in the pad of fat which surmounts the pelvic bone, and which was called the 'mount of Venus' (mons veneris) by the ancient anatomists, when they noted that it was most developed in the reproductive years. Both the labia, and more particularly the mons veneris, are covered with hair, the quantity of which varies from woman to woman. The pubic hair on the abdominal side of the mons veneris terminates in a straight line, whilst in the male the hair stretches upwards in an inverted 'V' to reach the umbilicus. The inner surfaces of the labia majora are free from hair, and are separated by a small groove from the thin labia minora, which guard the entrance to the vagina. The organism which causes syphilis may be transferred during sexual intercourse from an ulcer on the penis of the infected man and, entering through a tiny, invisible abrasion, form an ulcer on the inner surface of one or other of the labia majora.

The labia minora (the small lips) are delicate folds of skin which contain a little fatty tissue. They vary in size, and it was once believed that large labia minora were due to masturbation, which at that time was considered evil. It is now known that this is nonsense. In front, the labia minora split into two folds, one of which passes over, and the other under the clitoris, and at the back they join to form the fourchette, which is always torn during childbirth. In the reproductive years, the labia minora are hidden by the enlarged labia majora, but in childhood and old age the labia minora appear more prominent because the labia majora are relatively small.

The clitoris is the exact female equivalent of the male penis. The fold of the labia minora which passes over it is equivalent to the male foreskin (prepuce). It covers and protects the clitoris. The fold which passes under it is equivalent to the small band of tissue which joins the pink glans of the penis to the skin which covers it. It is called the frenulum. The clitoris is made up of erectile tissue, which fills with blood during sexual excitement. It is extremely sensitive to the touch. Orgasm in women occurs by the indirect stimulation of the clitoris by the movement of the penis in the vagina in sexual intercourse. It also occurs if the clitoris is gently stroked with the fingers or licked with the partner's tongue. The clitoris varies considerably in size, but is usually that of a green pea; as sexual excitement mounts, it increases in size. Once again this varies considerably between individuals.

The cleft below the clitoris and between the labia minora is called the vestibule (or entrance). Just below the clitoris is the external opening of that part of the urinary tract (the urethra) which connects the bladder to the outside world. The urethra in a woman is quite short, and several small side tubes, called Skene's ducts, open into it. The lining membrane of the urethra and its ducts is thin and delicate. It is through this thin membrane that the germs causing gonorrhoea enter the body, being transferred during sexual intercourse from an infected partner. The tubes which form Skene's ducts are complex in shape, and if the gonococcus

25

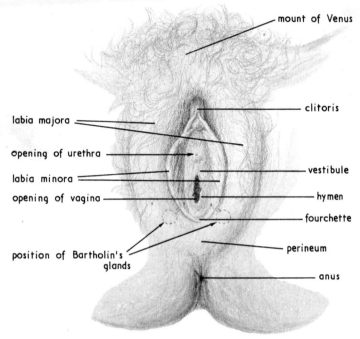

mount of Venus

clitoris

labia majora

opening of urethra

labia minora

opening of vagina

position of Bartholin's
glands

vestibule

hymen

fourchette

perineum

anus

*Fig. 2/1 The external genitals of a virgin.*

gets into these, the infection can linger on for a long time, unless it is adequately treated. In a woman this may be without any symptoms, but she is able to give gonorrhoea to any man with whom she has sexual intercourse.

Below the external urethral orifice is the hymen, which surrounds the vaginal orifice. The hymen is a thin, incomplete fold of membrane, which has one or more apertures in it. It varies considerably in shape and in elasticity, but is generally stretched or torn during the first attempt at sexual intercourse. The tearing is usually followed by a minute amount of bleeding. In many cultures the rupture of the

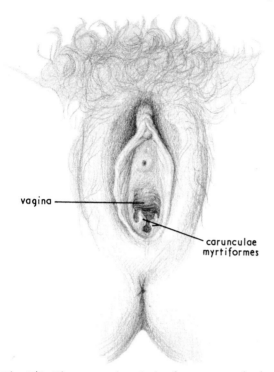

vagina

carunculae
myrtiformes

*Fig. 2/2. The external genitals of a woman who has had a child.*

hymen (also called the maidenhead), and the consequent
bleed, was considered a sign that the girl was a virgin at
the time of marriage, and the bed was inspected on the
morning after the first night of the honeymoon for evidence
of blood. Although an 'intact' hymen is considered a sign
of virginity, it is not a reliable sign, as in some cases coitus
fails to cause a tear, and in others the hymen may have
been torn previously by exploring fingers, either of the girl
herself or of a consort. The stretching and tearing of the
hymen at a first copulation may be painful, particularly if

27

the partners are apprehensive or ignorant of sexual matters. If the couple are well adjusted, the discomfort is minimal. Childbirth causes a much greater tearing of the hymen, and after delivery only a few tags remain. They are called carunculae myrtiformes (Fig. 2/2). Just outside the hymen, still within the vestibule but deep beneath the skin, are two collections of erectile tissue which fill with blood during sexual arousal. Deep in the backward part of the vestibule are two pea-sized glands which also secrete fluid during sexual arousal and moisten the entrance to the vagina, so that the penis may more readily enter it without discomfort. These glands occasionally become infected. They are known as Bartholin's glands. Like the urethra, Bartholin's glands are lined with a thin delicate membrane. Once again, the organisms causing gonorrhoea may enter a woman's body by invading Bartholin's glands.

The part of the vulva between the posterior fourchette and the anus, and the muscles which lie under the skin, forms a pyramid-shaped wedge of tissue separating the vagina and the rectum. It is called the perineum, and is of considerable importance in childbirth.

The vagina is a muscular tube which stretches upwards and backwards from the vestibule to reach the uterus. As well as being muscular, it contains a well-developed network of veins which become distended in sexual arousal. Normally the walls of the vagina lie close together, the vagina being a potential cavity which is distended by intravaginal tampons during menstruation, by the penis at copulation and by the infant during childbirth, when it stretches very considerably to permit the baby to be born. The vagina is about 9 cm ($3\frac{3}{4}$ in.) long, and at the upper end the cervix (or neck) of the uterus projects into it (Fig. 2/3). The vagina

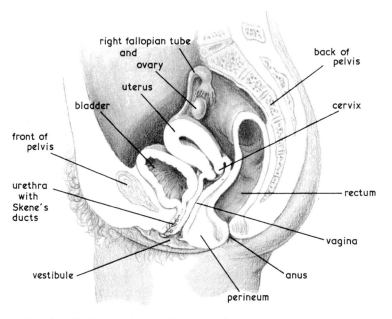

*Fig. 2/3. The internal genital organs of a woman.*

lies between the bladder in front and the rectum (or back-
passage) behind. At the sides it is surrounded and protected
by the strong muscles of the floor of the pelvis. Unless the
vagina has been damaged, injured or tightened at operation,
or has not developed due to an absence of sex hormones,
its size is quite adequate for sexual intercourse. A woman
who menstruates has a normal-sized vagina, and 'difficulty'
at intercourse is not due to her being 'small made'. This
is a myth. The cause lies not in the vagina, but in a mental
fear of sexual intercourse which leads the woman to tighten
the muscles which support the vagina to such an extent that
coitus is painful.

29

The vagina is a remarkable organ. Not only is it capable of great distension, but it keeps itself clean. The cells which form its walls are 30 cells deep, lying on each other like the bricks of a house wall. In the reproductive years, the top layer of cells is constantly being shed into the vagina, where the cells are acted upon by a small bacillus which normally lives there, to produce lactic acid. The lactic acid then kills any contaminating germs which may happen to get into the vagina. Because of this, 'cleansing' vaginal douches, so popular at one time in the U.S.A., are unnecessary. In childhood, the wall of the vagina is thin, and the production of lactic acid does not take place. However this is of little importance, because the vagina is not usually contaminated at this age. In old age, the lining becomes thin once again, and few cells are shed. Because of this, little or no lactic acid is formed, and contaminating germs may grow. This sometimes results in inflammation of the vagina.

The uterus is an even more remarkable organ than the vagina. Before pregnancy it is pear-shaped, averages 9 cm (3¾ in.) in length, 6 cm (2½ in.) in width at its widest point, and weighs 60 g (2 oz.). In pregnancy, it enlarges to weigh 1,000 g (2¼ lb.), and is able to contain a baby measuring 40 cm (17 in.) in length. It is able to undergo these changes because of the complex structure of its muscle and its exceptional response to the female sex hormones. The uterus is a hollow, muscular organ, which is located in the middle of the bony pelvis, lying between the bladder in front and the bowel behind (Fig. 2/3). It is pear-shaped, and its muscular front and back walls bulge into the cavity which is normally narrow and slit-like, until pregnancy occurs. Viewed from in front, the cavity is triangular, and is lined with a special tissue made up of glands in a

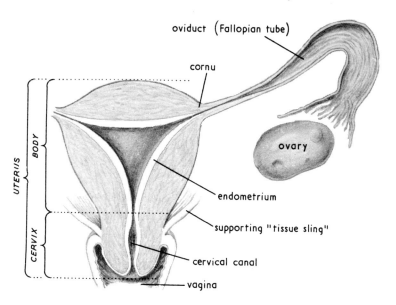

*Fig. 2/4. The cavity of the uterus viewed from the front.*

network of cells. This tissue is called the endometrium, and it undergoes changes during each menstrual cycle. For descriptive purposes, the uterus is divided into an upper part, or body, and a lower portion, or cervix uteri. The word cervix means neck, so that 'cervix uteri' means the neck of the womb. The cavity is narrow in the cervix, where it is called the cervical canal; widest in the body of the uterus; and then narrows again towards the cornu (or horn), where the cavity is continuous with the hollow of the Fallopian tube (Fig. 2/4). The cervix projects into the upper part of the vagina, and is a particular place where cancer sometimes develops.

The cervix is also often infected by the sexually transmissible diseases. The ulcer, which forms after infection by syphilis, may occur on the cervix, where it is invisible. Since it is also painless, the woman may not know that she has been infected. This has two dangers. First, she doesn't obtain treatment and has the risk of developing, years later, the serious, disabling third stage complications of syphilis; and second, she may infect her next sexual partner.

The canal of the cervix is lined with a delicate membrane, similar to that of the urethra and Bartholin's gland. As might be expected, gonorrhoea can invade a woman's body through the cervical canal.

Normally the uterus lies bent forward at an angle of 90° to the vagina, resting on the bladder. As the bladder fills, it rotates backwards; as it empties, the uterus falls forward. In about 10 per cent of women the uterus lies bent backwards. This is called retroversion. In the past it was considered a serious condition, causing backache, sterility and many other complaints. There were many operations for its cure. Today it is known that in most cases a retroverted uterus is of no consequence and is not the cause of the symptoms which were attributed to it in the past. However if gonorrhoea spreads upwards through the uterus it may cause pelvic infection, and a painful retroverted uterus.

The oviducts (or Fallopian tubes) are two small, hollow tubes, one on each side, which stretch for about 10 cm (4 in.) from the upper part of the uterus to lie in contact with the ovary on each side. The outer end of each oviduct is divided into long finger-like processes, and it is thought that these sweep up the egg when it is expelled from the ovary. The oviduct is lined with cells shaped like goblets, which lie between cells with frond-like borders. The oviduct is of great importance, as it is within it that fertilization of the egg takes place, and it is likely that its secretions help to nourish the fertilized egg as it is moved by the cells with long fronds towards the uterus. One of the complications of gonorrhoea is that the infection can spread into the oviducts, which become inflamed and may be damaged, so that the egg is prevented from being fertilized, and the woman is made permanently sterile.

The two ovaries are ovoid-shaped organs, averaging 3·5 cm ($1\frac{1}{2}$ in.) in length and 2 cm ($\frac{3}{4}$ in.) in breadth. In the infant they are small, delicate, thin structures, but after puberty they enlarge to reach the adult proportions mentioned. After the menopause, they become small and wrinkled, and in old age are less than half their adult size. Each ovary has a centre made up of small cells and a mesh of blood vessels. Surrounding this is the ovary proper – the cortex – which contains about 200,000 egg cells lying in a cellular bed (the stroma), and outside again, protecting the egg cells and the ovarian stroma, is a thickened layer of tissue. The ovaries are the equivalent of the male testes, and in addition to containing the egg cells on which all human life depends, are a hormone factory producing the female sex hormones, which are so important.

As can be appreciated, the passage within the genital tract extends from the vestibule, along the vagina, through the cervix and uterus, and along the tubes to the ovaries. It is because of this that the male spermatozoa can reach the female egg for fertilization to take place within the oviduct. It also permits infection to spread from the vagina to the ovaries, and beyond to cause peritonitis.

# man

In sexual intercourse, the man inserts his erect penis deeply into the woman's vagina, and with a thrusting movement reaches orgasm and ejaculates. If he is a good considerate lover, he will also seek to bring his female partner to orgasm. But if she inconsiderately has gonorrhoea or syphilis, or one of the lesser sexually transmitted diseases, his penis is likely to be infected during sexual intercourse.

The external genitals of a man consist of his penis and his two testicles, which lie in the scrotum between his legs, below the root of his penis.

Normally the penis is flaccid and hangs down slackly (Fig. 2/5). In the average adult male it measures 6 to 14 cm (2½–6

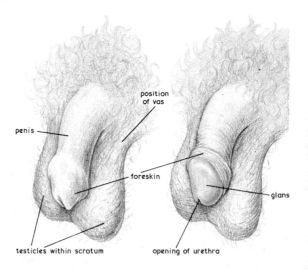

*Fig. 2/5. The uncircumcised penis and scrotum (foreskin retracted on the right).*

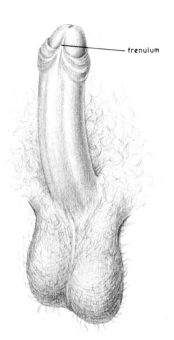

frenulum

*Fig. 2/6. The erect penis showing the glans penis and the frenulum.*

inches) in length, but as in every human characteristic, there is wide range of normality. When aroused sexually or by direct stimulation, the penis becomes full of blood, stiff, thicker and points erectly upwards. When this occurs a small penis undergoes a greater increase in size than does a large penis, so that the difference in size between erect penises is not great (Fig. 2/6).

If a man has not been circumcised, his foreskin peels back slightly, when his penis is erect, to expose the tip of the underlying head of the penis, which is called the glans penis. The glans is covered with a delicate mucous membrane (similar to that of the mouth) which is richly provided with sensitive nerve receptors. In sexual intercourse,

35

the foreskin peels back so that the entire glans penis is exposed to stimulation as the man thrusts forwards and backwards with his penis in the woman's vagina. Orgasm and ejaculation occur because the glans is stimulated by the touch of the vagina in sexual intercourse, or by the hand in masturbation.

The foreskin is prevented from peeling back completely by a band of tissue on the under surface of the glans, called the frenulum. This band of tissue starts just below the opening of the urethra, which is also called the 'eye' of the penis, and runs back in a small cleft in the glans. The frenulum is also extremely sensitive to touch.

Circumcision, or removal of the foreskin, is done in certain races and in certain religions. The Jews circumcise their boys on the eighth day of life to fulfil Abraham's covenant with God; the Muslims circumcise their boys at puberty as a symbol of reaching manhood; Aboriginal tribes in the Australian desert circumcise their boys, partly ceremonially as an initiation to manhood, partly for hygiene as the desert sand can irritate the foreskin. Circumcision of males has a long religious tradition; but in modern times, in the U.S.A. and Australia particularly, it has become a routine performance, not for religious reasons, but because it is the custom. It is said that mothers demand it, doctors profit by it, and babies cannot complain about it. The reasons given are that removal of the foreskin makes the penis cleaner, prevents masturbation, makes it less sensitive so that ejaculation is delayed in coitus, prevents cancer of the cervix in women, and prevents cancer of the penis in men. The evidence for all these arguments, except the last, is very shaky. The normal foreskin is adherent to the glans of the penis until the infant is a year old. After this time, it can be drawn back, and if the boy is taught to do this, he can keep his foreskin clean. It will not fix his mind on sex. Nor does the absence of a foreskin prevent masturbation, which anyhow is a normal activity. Circumcision does not improve a man's sexual performance, nor does it decrease it: it has no effect. There is no evidence, at all, that secretions which may be found under the foreskin cause cancer of the cervix in women, although many researchers have tried to prove this. The only men who develop cancer of the foreskin are those who are unhygienic. If, when children, they have been taught to draw back the foreskin and to clean it, cancer will not occur.

None of the so-called medical reasons for circumcision is valid, and there is strong evidence that the foreskin protects the glans of the penis, which is a delicate, sensitive structure.

The organism causing syphilis usually gains entry to the body of a man through tiny, invisible abrasions in the foreskin, or the skin covering the penis, or through abrasions in the delicate membrane which covers the glans penis, or the frenulum. At the site of infection an ulcer develops.

The urethra, in the male, is much longer than in the female, measuring about 18 cm (8 in.). It is 'S-shaped' and extends along the under-surface of the penis, through the prostate gland to reach the bladder. Along its course small side tunnels run into small glands. These are called Skene's ducts, and are identical with the Skene's ducts which enter a woman's urethra. And, as in woman, the urethra and its accessory glands are lined with a single layer of delicate membrane, through which the gonococcus can easily penetrate (Fig. 2/7).

The gonococcal infection may spread along the urethra

37

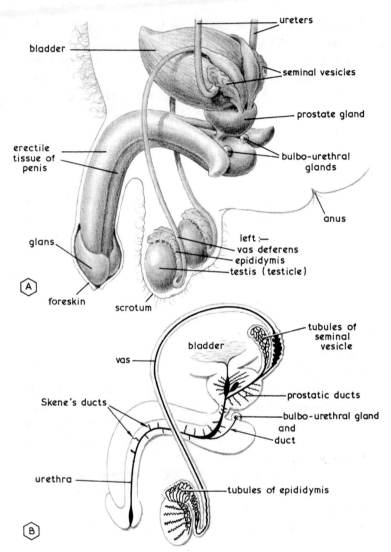

*Fig. 2/7. The external and internal genital organs of a man.*

38

and gain entry to the prostate gland which lies just below the bladder. The prostate gland is shaped like a chestnut, and has about 30 tiny ducts which join the urethra, and from which secretions of the prostate enter the urethra. Just behind the prostate, one on each side, are the seminal vesicles. The seminal vesicle is a blind pouch which develops from each vas deferens. This is a tube which stretches from each testis to the urethra, and along which the sperms pass. The seminal vesicles are so called because it was believed that they stored semen, although now it is known that they only store the sticky fluid which forms most of the ejaculate, and which nourishes the spermatozoa.

As I mentioned, the two vas deferens stretch from the testicles to the urethra. For the first quarter of their length they are outside the body in the scrotum. If you grasp, gently, the scrotum where it joins the body and with the thumb in front and the forefinger behind roll the tissues, you will feel a cord-like structure. This is the vas deferens.

As well as permitting the sperms to reach the penis, the vas deferens also permits the gonococcus to reach the epididymis and the testicles. The epididymis is a long, twisted, narrow tube, like a tangled ball of string in which the sperms mature before they are ejaculated. It lies alongside and is fixed to its testicle. It connects with the vas above, and with the narrow tubules which make up most of the testis below (Fig. 2/8). The lining of the epididymis is very delicate and if infected by the gonococcus may become damaged and even blocked, which of course makes the man sterile. This is one of the unpleasant complications of untreated gonorrhoea in a man.

The two testes are smooth, oval structures, which are very tender if squeezed, and which lie one in each side of the

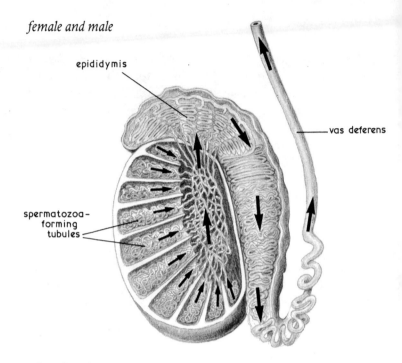

epididymis

vas deferens

spermatozoa–
forming
tubules

*Fig. 2/8. The epididymis and testis.*

scrotum. Each testicle is made up of about 250 small com-
partments, like the sections of an orange. Each com-
partment contains a twisted tube lined by cells. These cells
develop and form the spermatozoa from puberty onwards.
Between the convolutions of the tubes are special cells
which secrete the male hormone androgen.

It will be appreciated that in the male the genital tract,
at least from the prostate onwards, is used both by spermatozoa, during ejaculation, and by urine, during urination.
Because of this, infection can spread either to the bladder,
or to the testicle, with equal ease. This applies particularly
to gonococcal infections.

# 3

# about

# gonorrhoea

Case – 74. John H-, aged 21, first attended the clinic on the evening of 22nd April. He complained of a burning feeling when he passed urine, and of a discharge from his penis. He said that he had been out at the pub four days before, and had met a girl. They had gone off together, and had sexual intercourse at her parents' home. Her parents were away. He had known the girl before, but had never previously had sexual intercourse with her. Examination of the discharge showed the presence of *Neisseria gonorrhoeae*. John H- had gonorrhoea. He was treated, and it was stressed to him that he must continue to attend the clinic for three months, so that it could be made sure that the gonorrhoea was cured, and so that tests could be made to find out if he also had acquired syphilis. Meanwhile a social worker visited the girl, and induced her to come for investigation and treatment. During the investigation of her contacts, four other men were traced who had been infected by her, and they had infected two other girls. As far as is known all contacts were traced, with the exception of the man who had given the infection to the first girl. He was a serviceman whom the girl had picked up – although she claimed he had picked her up – at a cinema. They had gone to a coffee-bar after the film, and later had had sexual intercourse, on the river bank. She did not know his full name, nor where he was stationed.

*e*

As old as recorded history, gonorrhoea has been a by-blow of sexual intercourse. It was mentioned by the Jews in Leviticus, the third book of Moses, and the name of the disease, gonorrhoea, was coined by the ancient Greek physician Galen, in 130 A.D. The word means 'flow of seed', and the term graphically describes the main feature of the disease.

Gonorrhoea is an acute infection of the genito-urinary tract, and is almost always spread from person to person by sexual intercourse. In very rare cases it is spread by other methods. One example is the spread of gonorrhoea from an infected mother to the eyes of her infant during childbirth. It is one of the commonest infectious diseases, and it has been estimated that more than 200 million new cases occur each year.

The organism which causes gonorrhoea is a small bean-shaped germ, called *Neisseria gonorrhoeae*, which is transferred during sexual intercourse from the urethra of an infected man to the urethra, or to the cervix, of his female partner, or to the rectum of his male partner, if he is homosexual. It is transferred with equal facility from the urethra, the cervix or the Bartholin glands of an infected woman to the urethra of an uninfected male partner during sexual intercourse. The urethra, the cervix and the rectum are lined with a single layer of cells, which the gonococcus finds easy to penetrate, and having established a base, it multiplies very quickly. The vagina, which is lined by several layers of cells, is not affected, as the gonococcus is unable to penetrate this 'wall of cells'.

The *Neisseria gonorrhoeae*, or gonococcus, is a very fragile organism, and dies very rapidly if it is not within the warm human body. Small falls in temperature will kill it, and even if the infected discharge from the urethra contaminates clothes or other articles, those articles are rarely infectious, as drying quickly kills the gonococcus. For this reason the story that you can get gonorrhoea from an infected towel, a lavatory seat, or infected clothing should be remembered for what it is – a story! Very occasionally a parent or an attendant who has acute gonorrhoea may transfer the germs, by their hands, to the vagina of a young girl, and cause gonorrhoea in the child. This only occurs if the parent first fingers his or her own urethra and then fingers the child's vulva. The wall of the vagina of a girl before she reaches puberty is only one or two cells thick, so that the gonococcus can penetrate it. But it should be stressed that this is a very rare method of catching gonorrhoea, and the most usual method, by far, is by having sexual intercourse with an infected partner.

A man knows he is infected between 3 and 5 days after sexual intercourse. The first thing he notices is that he has developed discomfort or tingling in his urethra. Very quickly a discharge appears which is creamy, thick and purulent, and which drips from his penis (Fig. 3/1). He also finds that it is uncomfortable to pass urine and when he does, he has a burning feeling in his urethra. The area around the 'eye' of his penis is reddened, but he usually feels quite well apart from the symptoms I have mentioned. If he does not seek treatment, the infection spreads upwards along his urethra and in 10 to 14 days the part of the urethra nearest to his bladder becomes inflamed. When this happens, the burning and pain on passing urine increase, and he may feel unwell, with headaches, or with fever from absorption into his blood of toxic products from the infection.

drip of pus

*Fig. 3/1. Gonorrhoeal urethral discharge.*

If he still does not seek treatment, the symptoms disappear in a few more days, or the disease spreads to involve organs which are adjacent to the urethra, particularly the prostate gland and the bladder, or even to the testicle, where it causes an acute inflammation with a painful, swollen testicle, and the chance of permanent damage which could cause sterility.

In the days before the antibiotics were available, the only treatment for gonorrhoea was the use of local antiseptics. These were not very efficient and may have aggravated, rather than cured, the disease. In those days, the symptoms of chronic gonorrhoea developed. The most common, and most painful one, was a narrowing, or stricture, of the posterior urethra. This led to difficulty in passing urine, or to the failure to pass urine at all. The treatment was painful, and consisted of pushing narrow metal, or plastic, rods along the urethra to try and stretch the narrowed portion. The operation was called dilatation of the urethral stricture, and the sufferer had to submit to this at frequent intervals.

In women the pattern of the progress of gonorrhoea is more sinister and more serious. In the first place, between 30 and 50 per cent of infected women have no symptoms, but they can transmit the disease for prolonged periods. They act as a silent reservoir of infection, which considerably complicates the control of gonorrhoea, for a promiscuous woman who has symptomless gonorrhoea can infect a large number of men. Even when women develop symptoms these are usually less marked than in men. This is because a woman's urethra is much shorter, and is more readily cleaned by passing urine. In fact, one recommended method of avoiding gonorrhoea was to empty the bladder immediately after sexual intercourse. It was not very efficient. The other was for the man to wear a condom when he sought casual sex. This is a more efficient prophylactic method, but certainly does not give complete protection.

If a woman unknowingly harbours the gonococcus, or knowing she has gonorrhoea, fails to have treatment, the disease may spread in several directions within her body. One common, and painful, complication is if one of Bartholin's glands becomes infected. These glands lie deep in the tissues at the entrance of the vulva, and supply secretions which make the vagina moist and sexual intercourse more pleasant. If one of the glands becomes infected with gonorrhoea, it becomes swollen, painful and tender.

Occasionally the gonococcus spreads upwards from the cervix, through the uterine cavity, to infect the oviducts, or Fallopian tubes (Fig. 3/2). This seems to occur during

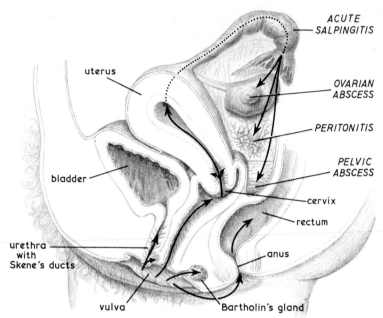

ACUTE
SALPINGITIS

OVARIAN
ABSCESS

PERITONITIS

PELVIC
ABSCESS

cervix

rectum

anus

Bartholin's gland

uterus

bladder

urethra
with
Skene's ducts

vulva

*Fig. 3/2. The spread of gonorrhoea.*

menstruation, and if the tubes become infected the woman complains of fever, headache and pain in her lower abdomen. Examination, particularly pelvic examination, by a doctor causes considerable pain. The sinister sequel of infection of the oviducts, which is termed salpingitis, is that the tubes may become kinked and blocked causing permanent sterility. If this happens in adolescence, following a chance sexual encounter with an infected male, it may prevent the woman ever having a child when she marries.

In both sexes, gonorrhoea may involve the anus and rectum. In women this occurs either following anal intercourse by an infected man, or when the infected secretions con-

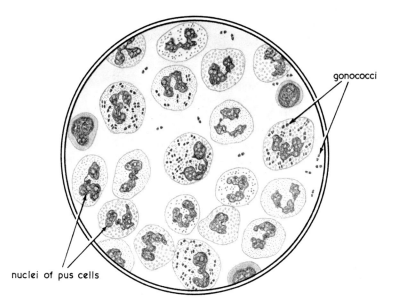

*Fig. 3/3. The gonococcus seen through the microscope.*

taminate the anus during sleep or after defaecation. In males, the infection follows anal intercourse with an infected homosexual partner. In one surprising study, made in Denmark, 30 per cent of women with gonorrhoea also had anal infection.

Gonorrhoea is diagnosed, in the male, by taking a specimen of the urethral discharge, and placing it on a slide. After appropriate staining, the slide is examined under a microscope, when clusters of bean-shaped gonococci, which seem to prefer to lie in pairs, are found inside pus cells (Fig. 3/3). In women, the diagnosis is often more difficult and smears are usually taken from the woman's urethra, her upper vagina, and her cervix when gonorrhoea is suspected. These smears are placed on special glass dishes which

47

contain a nutrient material and the dishes are heated, or incubated, for two days. In this way any gonococci present will grow, and the growth will be seen on the material in the dish. If a specimen from this material is now examined under a microscope the typical bean-shaped germs of gonorrhoea can be identified.

Once the diagnosis has been made, the patient is told by the doctor that he (or she) has gonorrhoea and his help is sought in contacting the sexual partner who gave him the disease. Until the disease is cured the patient must avoid alcohol, as this seems to encourage the disease to relapse, and must obviously avoid sexual intercourse, for he will certainly infect his next partner. He should wash his hands after passing urine, or defaecating, and should wash his genitals each day with soap and water, drying them with a towel which nobody else uses.

The patient is then given treatment. Today penicillin is the most efficient killer of gonococci, although increasing numbers are becoming relatively resistant to penicillin, so that higher and higher doses are needed to cure the disease. The reason for resistance is not clear, but it may be due to the abuse of penicillin, given in inadequate doses for inappropriate, or trivial, disorders over the past 20 years. Another reason, particularly in Asia, is that many prostitutes are given a weekly injection of penicillin, supposedly to protect their clients from getting venereal disease. The dose is too low to eliminate gonorrhoea from their bodies, and the surviving resistant germs are readily transferred. A particularly resistant strain of gonorrhoea is the gift of the South Vietnamese prostitutes to their allies, which the soldiers have gratuitously exported to the U.S.A. and Australia, and which has infected girls in those two nations.

48

Perhaps it is just retribution for the U.S. and Australian involvement in Vietnam, and the partial destruction of that nation.

By 1972, in many nations, between 20 and 30 per cent of all cases of gonorrhoea were relatively resistant to normal doses of penicillin. It has also become increasingly obvious that the more simple the treatment the more effective it is. This has meant that new strategies have had to be developed.

Penicillin remains the treatment of choice for gonorrhoea, but medical research has discovered that penicillin is more effective in killing resistant gonococci if another drug is given at the same time. The usual method in the treatment of gonorrhoea is for the patient to take two tablets of this drug, called probenecid, either an hour before or at the time of receiving the penicillin, and a further tablet, 6, 12 and 18 hours later. Probenecid blocks the excretion of penicillin by the kidneys and so enables higher levels to be obtained in the blood. This gives penicillin a more lethal effect on the gonococcus. The penicillin is given as a single injection into a muscle, or else the patient takes a number of capsules by mouth all at one go. In women who have gonorrhoea, and homosexual men who have a gonococcal infection of the rectum, a second injection of penicillin is sometimes given on the next day, and the patient takes the probenecid tablets every six hours for two days. During treatment the doctor also takes a sample of blood to check for syphilis.

In most cases this cures the patient, but since gonorrhoea may lurk in the body it is essential that every patient re-attends the doctor or the hospital clinic for follow-up. Seven days after receiving the penicillin the patient passes a specimen of urine which is examined by the doctor, who also takes further smears from the urethra (and from the cervix if the patient is a woman). In the case of homosexual men, specimens are taken from the rectum for examination. The smears are examined under a microscope and 'cultured' to make sure that no gonococci are still present. Between one-tenth and one-quarter of men treated for gonorrhoea develop a urethral discharge between five and 25 days after receiving treatment. This is due to another sexually transmitted disease, which was caught by the man at the time he caught gonorrhoea. It is called non-specific urethritis and is discussed in Chapter 6.

Smears are taken at weekly intervals for three weeks after the penicillin injection. If any of them show that gonorrhoea is still present, a second course of antibiotics is given. A final check is made three months after the disease was diagnosed. Smears are again made, and a sample of the person's blood is tested for syphilis. If no gonococci are found, and the blood test is negative for syphilis, the patient is considered cured.

Some people are allergic to penicillin. Luckily, other antibiotics are available which they can take, but the follow-up tests are made in exactly the same way.

Because gonorrhoea is 'silent' in so many women, and because of its unpleasant consequences both to the woman herself and her sexual partners, an even more careful follow-up has to be made after a woman has been treated for gonorrhoea. She requires to be re-examined five to seven days after completing treatment when smears are taken from her urethra, her vagina and her cervix. These are repeated in the first days after her next two menstrual periods. If the tests are negative at each examination a woman can be sure that she has been cured of gonorrhoea.

# 4

# about

# syphilis

Case – 73. Kevin P-, who was aged 18 when he first attended the clinic, presented with an obvious chancre on his penis. He gave a history of having acquired the infection during his recent holiday, from a casual acquaintance whom he had met on the beach. He and a group of friends had driven to the seaside resort for a week's holiday of fun, sun and perhaps sex. At this time Kevin had not had sexual intercourse. The group had picked up, or been picked up by, three girls, and after spending most of the afternoon with them had driven out to a drive-in cafe for hot dogs and coke. They had then driven to the sand hills, and each of the six men had had sexual intercourse with one or other of the girls. Three weeks later, on his return home, Kevin had noticed a small pimple on his penis which grew and spread over the next few days. During this time the edge of the lump became thick and hard, and the centre soft, so that it resembled a button felt through a layer of cloth. The centre of the lump then broke down, ulcerating, and exposing a raw red base which oozed a clear fluid. At the same time glands in Kevin's groins became swollen and felt like round pieces of rubber under the skin. At this point in time, he sought medical attention at the hospital.

The doctor who examined him had no doubt that the ulcer was syphilitic, but to confirm his clinical impression he took a swab. He first cleaned the ulcer with a weak salt solution, then squeezed each side of it for a few moments, so that clear fluid welled up from its red base. Surprisingly,

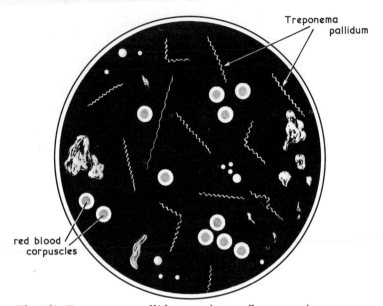

Treponema
pallidum

red blood
corpuscles

*Fig. 4/1.* Treponema pallidum *and pus cells seen under a microscope.*

to Kevin, this was quite painless. The fluid was placed on two glass slides and examined under a 'dark ground' microscope. This confirmed the clinical diagnosis.

Viewed down the microscope, the organisms causing syphilis, the *Treponema pallidum*, were seen as corkscrew-shaped objects which glistened bluish-white as they moved, twisting on themselves (Fig. 4/1). Occasionally they bent to a right angle and then snapped straight. Occasionally their coils contracted and then expanded so that they looked like animated watch springs.

The doctor explained that syphilis was curable but that Kevin would require to continue to visit the clinic after the ulcer had healed, so that blood tests could be taken to make sure that he was really cured. These tests would be made at regular intervals for a year. The doctor stressed the great importance to Kevin's future health, of having the blood tests made.

Kevin was also asked the names of his friends and of the girls so that social workers could contact them and induce them to be examined, to have blood tests and if they were found to have syphilis to be given treatment.

Syphilis is an infectious disease which is spread by sexual contact, so that it is contagious as well as infectious. The organism which causes syphilis is a tiny slender corkscrew-shaped organism, which is invisible to the naked eye. It measures about 20μ in length. A μ, pronounced mew, is one-thousandth of a millimetre in length, so that 500 organisms placed end to end would be needed to measure one centimetre, or 1250 to measure an inch. The organism is called *Treponema pallidum,* and it is coiled along its 20μ length. Usually there are about twelve coils. The *Treponema pallidum* can only live in the moist warm atmosphere of the human body, and dies within a very few hours outside it. But once inside the body it thrives.

When Kevin was infected by the girl, 1000 or more treponemes entered his body through a tiny, invisible break in the pink surface mucous membrane of his penis. Within 30 hours, the number had doubled, and doubled again every 30 hours, so that by the time he visited the doctor there were at least 10,000 million treponemes in his body.

Within 30 minutes of being infected, the organism had spread to the lymph glands in his groins, where they were filtered for a short time. They then invaded his blood stream, and were carried throughout his body. Without treatment the organisms chronically infect almost all the tissues of the body and over the years invade and damage them.

However the organisms do not have it all their own way. The *Treponema pallidum* has a fatty shell, but inside it contains protein. When a 'foreign' protein is injected into, or inoculated into, the body (as is the case of infection by syphilis), the body reacts. The foreign protein stimulates certain blood cells to multiply, and these cells are sensitized to the particular protein, so that should a further infection occur they mobilize to attack the invader at its point of entry, rather in the way in which a country attacked by a foreign invader tries to immobilize the invading army on the beaches. Unfortunately in the first, or primary, infection by syphilis the body's defences are inadequate, and the treponemes are not contained so that they get into the blood stream and multiply rapidly.

It takes about three weeks for the defences to be mobilized, which is why the person who has been infected with syphilis has no symptoms or signs for three weeks. Then the sensitized blood cells attack the treponemes, which are still multiplying in the tissues of the beachhead – in this case the mucous membrane of the penis. This causes the first sign of syphilis, the raised pimple on the penis. In the next few days many of the treponemes are killed, as are many of the white blood cells, with the result that a zone of hard tissue develops around the pimple. It also leads to a reduction in blood supply to the pimple, so that its centre dies and sloughs off leaving an ulcer. In time the ulcer heals leaving a scar. This takes from three to eight weeks. Unfortunately in some cases the primary lesion, the ulcer, is quite

54

small, or is not even noticed, so that the infected person does not seek treatment.

At the same time as the white blood cells are being mobilized, the treponemes which have invaded the blood stream cause another reaction. They induce the blood to make a chemical substance called an antibody. The formation of antibody to the treponemes is a slow process, but four to eight weeks after the primary infection, it can be measured by taking a sample of blood from a vein. Once formed, the antibody to syphilis tends to persist for years unless the syphilis is cured, when it usually disappears from the blood over a period of about a year. The measurement of antibody is the basis of the blood tests to detect syphilis, which many States in the U.S.A. insist on making before a couple get married, and which are made in early pregnancy to make sure that the expectant mother is not carrying syphilis in her blood which may infect her unborn infant. They would also be made on all the contacts (who could be traced) of the girl who infected Kevin, to find how many of them had developed syphilis.

Syphilis is a sexually transmitted disease, and since most couples have genital sex, which implies that the man's penis is inserted into the woman's vagina, the primary lesion of syphilis, which is also called a chancre, usually develops on the penis or on the woman's vulva (Figs. 4/2 and 4/3). However in about 25 per cent of women, who are infected by a man with untreated syphilis, the primary lesion develops on her cervix and is invisible, but highly infectious should she have sexual intercourse with another, uninfected partner. Without treatment the person who has syphilis remains infectious for about two years, after which the chance diminishes and it is unusual for an untreated syphilitic

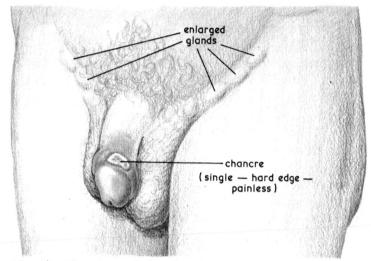

enlarged
glands

chancre
( single — hard edge —
painless )

*Fig. 4/2. The primary lesion of syphilis in a man – a chancre on the penis.*

to transmit the disease after five years have passed. But as will be seen, the disease continues to infect and to damage tissues in his body.

In 5 per cent of cases of primary syphilis, the lesion develops elsewhere than on the genitalia. Passive homo-sexuals, infected by a homosexual partner, may develop the chancre on the anus, or in the lower part of the rectum. Couples, whether homo- or heterosexual, who enjoy oral sex may develop the lesion on the lips, or tongue, if either partner is infectious.

Very rarely syphilis is acquired by means other than sexual intercourse. But these infections are so rare that in general they can be disregarded. Since the treponeme is so fragile when outside the human body and dies so rapidly, the story that you can pick up syphilis from a toilet seat

56

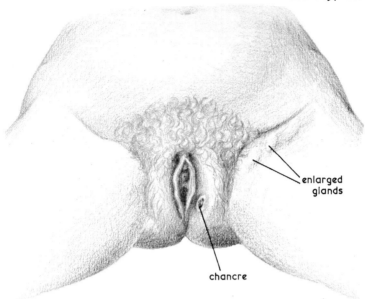

enlarged
glands

chancre

*Fig. 4/3. The primary lesion of syphilis in a woman – a chancre
on a labium, with enlarged lymph glands in the groin.*

is untrue. An old Professor of Medicine whom I once knew
was asked by a student if you can get syphilis in a lavatory.
'Yes,' he replied, 'You can, but it is a ridiculous and improper place in which to have sexual intercourse.'

Syphilis is a chronic disease which, in the course of its
untreated history, can infect almost any tissue of the body.
For the understanding of the disease it is customary to
divide it into three stages, primary, secondary and tertiary,
or late, syphilis.

Primary syphilis is the stage of the initial infection and
is first diagnosed clinically when the primary lesion, or
chancre, appears 10 to 90 days after the person is infected.
Most chancres develop in the period 20 to 25 days after

sexual intercourse with an infected partner. The primary lesion has been described already, but it is worth repeating that it usually develops on the penis or the vulva, is usually single, has a hard edge and ulcerated centre from which clear fluid oozes, and is painless. It is extremely infectious. A few days after the appearance of the primary lesion, the lymph glands in each groin enlarge to form painless rubbery masses. The primary lesion, if untreated, heals slowly over four to eight weeks usually leaving a small scar.

Throughout this time the treponemes in the blood have been multiplying and have been provoking the reaction of the body's defences. As the antibody defence is provoked, the level of antibody in the blood rises. When the primary lesion has been present for three weeks, about 50 per cent of people tested will have a positive blood test; by five weeks, 80 per cent will have a positive test and by ten weeks, if treatment has not been given, all infected persons will have a positive blood test.

Six to eight weeks after the primary lesion, the secondary stage of syphilis develops. Quite often the infected person feels 'off colour', and may have headaches, fever, sore throat or joint pains, although these symptoms are not very helpful in making a diagnosis. There are four main groups of lesions which suggest secondary syphilis, and all of the secondary lesions are very infectious. By the time they appear, the blood tests for syphilis have become positive in over 99 per cent of patients, so that diagnosis is easy if the patient is honest and helpful and the doctor alert.

The most common condition is a skin rash. More than 80 per cent of untreated patients have this. The rash starts as faint pale pink spots which appear first along the ribs and over the trunk but rapidly spread, to cover the back and

58

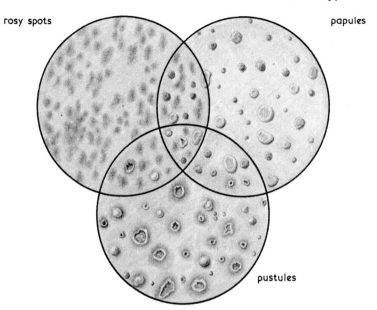

*Fig. 4/4. The secondary rash of syphilis.*

the belly, and appear on the face around the mouth and chin (Figs. 4/4 and 4/5). Occasionally the rash forms a band across the forehead, which the doctors of the eighteenth century called 'the crown of Venus', in a whimsical, if accurate, way. The spots, which are usually round, rapidly become dusky red, and as time passes may become pimply, and the centre of the pimple may shed its skin. They do not itch, but occasionally, if picked, become infected and form pus spots. The rash persists for about six weeks and then slowly fades, although it may reappear unless treatment has been given. In women, who sometimes have no visible primary lesions, the secondary skin rash may be the first sign to alert the doctor that the woman has syphilis.

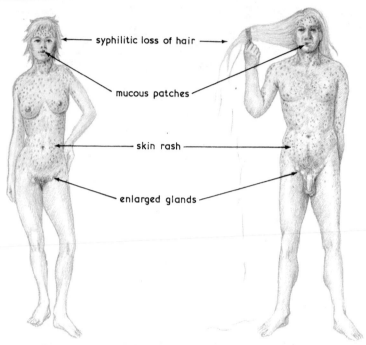

syphilitic loss of hair

mucous patches

skin rash

enlarged glands

*Fig. 4/5. The secondary stage of syphilis.*

The second common secondary lesion occurs in moist areas on the skin or on mucous membranes such as the mouth, the vulva and the anus. Because these areas are more delicate and moist, the secondary lesions of syphilis which develop on them are different. In the vulval area in women, or around the anus in either sex (Fig. 4/6), warty growths may appear. These have flat tops and are reddish or grey in colour. They are very infectious, and occasionally appear in other moist areas, such as between the buttocks or on the scrotum. In the mouth, in the vagina, or on the penis, small grey raised patches, looking like snail tracks

60

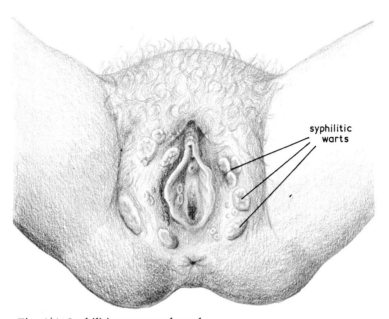

syphilitic
warts

*Fig. 4/6. Syphilitic warts on the vulva.*

may develop. These, too, are painless and very infectious. They are called mucous patches (Fig. 4/7). Mucous patches and syphilitic warts affect about 30 per cent of untreated syphilitics.

About 10 per cent of infected persons develop signs of meningitis with irritating, recurrent headaches.

The secondary lesions of syphilis last from three to 12 months and then disappear.

The third stage of syphilis may develop from two to 20 years after the disappearance of the secondary lesions. During this time the only indication that the patient has syphilis is that the blood test is positive. In many untreated patients the third stage fails to develop, although the person

61

*about syphilis*

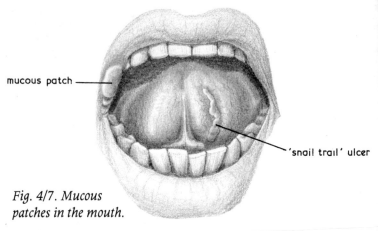

mucous patch

'snail trail' ulcer

*Fig. 4/7. Mucous
patches in the mouth.*

is at greater risk of dying than an uninfected person. Today, with effective treatment of early infectious syphilis, the lesions of the tertiary stage are increasingly less commonly encountered. In fact, we would not really know what happens to the untreated syphilitic were it not for a study in Oslo.

In the year 1891, Professor Brøck of Oslo, Norway, became convinced that the then current treatment of syphilis did nothing to cure the disease. At that time reliance was placed on mercury, which had first been suggested as a cure five centuries earlier. Mercury had been used for the treatment of leprosy since the twelfth century when it had been brought back from Palestine by the Crusaders. Used as an ointment – it was called Saracen's ointment – it was rubbed into the skin. It was not very effective in curing leprosy. As the manifestations of late syphilis resembled those of leprosy, so that the two diseases were often confused, mercury was introduced in the late 1400s for the treatment of syphilis. Four centuries later it was still the

62

mainstay of treatment, and as Professor Brøck observed, it was almost useless. In fact he argued, the toxic side-effects of mercury were so many, and the cure of syphilis by using mercury so uncertain, that the effects of the treatment were worse than those of the disease.

He decided, therefore, not to treat any patients who developed syphilis, but as he knew the disease was highly infectious in the early stages, he kept them in hospital until all traces of syphilis had disappeared. This took from three to 12 months. After that time the patients were free to go about their business, but were expected to keep in contact with him for the rest of their lives. In all, he gave no treatment to nearly 2000 patients over the 20-year-period up to 1910. By then, Paul Ehrlich had invented his 'magic bullet' against syphilis, which he called '606', or Salvarsan. As it contained arsenic, not mercury, Professor Brøck felt that he had to discontinue his experiment, and to use salvarsan on all new patients. But he continued to follow up his old, untreated patients.

The follow-up, through life, and by autopsy after death, of Professor Brøck's patients, shows the natural history of syphilis. The first observation was that in 24 per cent of the patients, a relapse occurred after the secondary lesions had cleared. The relapse occurred within two years of the primary infection in most patients, and 55 of the 244 patients who had one relapse had a second relapse. The nature of the relapse was that the lesions in the moist areas recurred, mainly in the mouth, in the throat, or around the anus. During the relapse the patient again became highly infectious to others. And then, for no reason, in about three to six months, the ulcers disappeared, and the patient was again cured.

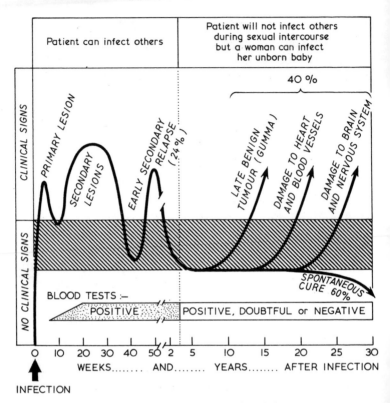

*Fig. 4/8. The natural history of untreated syphilis.*

The remainder of the observations were about late, or tertiary syphilis. These were made by Professor Brøck's successor, Dr. Bruusgaard, and by his successor, Dr. Danbolt. Nine hundred and fifty-three patients were followed to their death, or at least for forty years after they were first infected (Fig. 4/8). Sixty per cent of them had no further clinical evidence of the disease, although the treponemes were insidiously damaging their tissues. This is shown by mortality,

64

or death, statistics. The syphilitic patients had a greater chance of dying at an earlier age than non-syphilitic people. Death was more likely to occur to men between the ages of 40 and 49, when the extra chance of dying was 122 per cent higher than that of non-syphilitics; and to women between the ages of 30 and 49, when their extra chance of dying, over non-syphilitic women of a similar age, was 90 per cent. But at all ages the chance of death occurring to a syphilitic person was greater than to a non-syphilitic person. The untreated disease shortened a person's life, even if syphilis was not the cause of the death. In fact, syphilis was the direct cause of death in only one patient in ten.

Forty per cent of the untreated patients developed signs of late syphilis. These showed in three ways. In 15 per cent of cases, the patient developed a thickened ulcerating tumour, in or under the skin or in a bone. If the tumour, which was called a gumma, developed in the skin, the skin rotted away leaving a painful ulcer, which usually became infected (Fig. 4/9). If the gumma developed in a bone, usually a bone of the lower leg, or the skull, was affected. The patient complained of a deep, gnawing, boring pain which was worse at night and went on and on.

In about 10 per cent of cases, damage to the heart or great blood vessels appeared from 10 to 30 years after the primary infection. This form of the disease affected men twice as often as women, and was thought to occur more frequently amongst heavy manual workers. If the heart was involved, the patient developed chest pain and shortness of breath. If the great vessels were involved he often had no symptoms, but was likely to drop dead suddenly when his aorta ruptured.

Ten per cent of the Oslo patients developed syphilis of

65

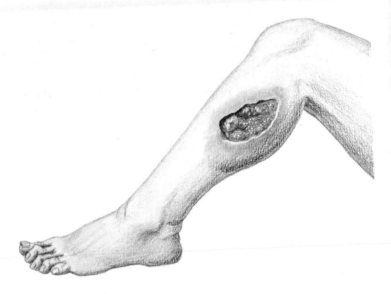

*Fig. 4/9. A gumma on the leg.*

the brain or spinal cord. This occurred from five to 35 years after the initial infection. Once again, more men than women were affected in this particularly horrible way. The disease showed as mental decay, and at autopsy, the brain of the victim was shrunken. First the person's memory worsened, then his concentration became less and he developed a lack of judgement. Then, in succession, he lost emotional control, so that he would fall into episodes of weeping, or of rage, for no reason. Finally he developed delusions, either of grandeur or of guilt, or he became demented and apathetic.

If the spinal cord was affected, he developed tabes dorsalis, when he had fleeting sharp pains in his shins, as if someone had beaten his legs with the back of an axe, and developed an unsteady swaying gait which was worse at night. Both of these symptoms progressed as the years went by, until the patient was only able to walk with the help of a stick, and eventually became bed-ridden, incontinent of urine and sometimes blind. In the last stages, violent episodes of gut pain and vomiting occurred, as did severe pain in the rectum, in the bladder or in the penis.

Today, with adequate treatment of the early stages of syphilis, the third stage lesions are increasingly rare, but they cause so much misery that a person who thinks he might have syphilis should be tested, and if he is found to have the disease, he should be treated adequately, so that he infects no other person, and so that he avoids the lesions of tertiary syphilis, and the greater likelihood of premature death which affects the untreated syphilitic.

Syphilis can be transmitted from an infected woman to her unborn baby long after she has ceased to be able to transmit the disease to men during sexual intercourse. This is because the treponemes continue to multiply in her blood stream. But it is true that the more recently she has acquired syphilis, the greater is the chance that her unborn baby will be affected. The treponemes manage to penetrate the placenta, or afterbirth, which separates the baby from its mother and then infect the baby. Because of the character of the placenta, penetration only occurs in the second half of pregnancy, after the end of the 20th week from the time of the last menstrual period. This means that if blood tests are made in the first 10 weeks of pregnancy on all pregnant women, those women who have had syphillis which was not properly treated, and those who have contracted syphilis, and do not know it, can be treated with penicillin before the baby is affected. This means that the baby will be completely healthy.

In most rich countries all pregnant women are routinely tested for syphilis. Fortunately the number of women who have syphilis is few, and in Britain, for example, only one in every 2000 antenatal patients has a positive test. But the test is worth doing because of the damage untreated syphilis causes to the unborn baby and because the baby is the innocent victim of its mother's disease. About one quarter of infected unborn babies die in the womb and the mother delivers a dead, swollen, skin peeling, bloated baby. The remaining 75 per cent of infected babies are born alive, but one quarter die early in life if no treatment is given. Of the remainder, half develop the signs of tertiary syphilis between the age of 7 and 15.

The progress of the disease in the infant is the same as that in the infected adult. The primary stage takes place whilst the baby is in its mother's womb. The secondary stage is present at birth or becomes noticeable within six weeks of birth. The skin rashes are particularly common and highly infectious (Fig. 4/10) but the infant's nose and throat may also be involved and mucous patches may develop, so that the child whines and snuffles. A few infants develop swellings in the ends of their bones, especially the long bones of their legs. If the leg is moved the child screams with pain. In 10 per cent of children infected in the womb, the trepomenes invade the child's brain, and this may lead to convulsions and mental deficiency.

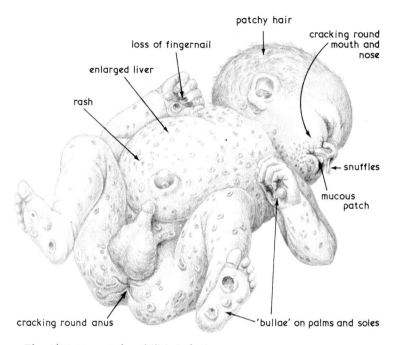

patchy hair

cracking round
mouth and
nose

loss of fingernail

enlarged liver

rash

← snuffles

mucous
patch

cracking round anus

'bullae' on palms and soles

*Fig. 4/10. Prenatal syphilitic infection.*

If the infant is treated in early life it will be cured, but if it is not tertiary syphilis may develop when the child is aged between 7 and 15. Rarely it occurs earlier, or later in adult life. As in the adult three lesions are common. The first are gummas, which form especially in the cartilage of the child's nose, or the palate of his mouth, and may cause collapse of the bridge of the nose. They also tend to develop in the bones of the lower leg. This causes a painful swelling and deformity of the leg. In 25 to 50 per cent of prenatally infected children, the disease damages the cornea of the eyes. It starts with pain in the eye, particularly when the

69

child looks at a bright light, and he complains of mistiness of vision. The episode lasts for a few weeks and then goes. The attacks recur, and with each, the person's sight is diminished, so that blindness eventually occurs.

Finally, between 10 and 15 per cent of untreated prenatally infected syphilitics develop mental damage, with the mental changes already described.

The tragedy of the so-called 'congenital syphilitic' (that is, the child infected whilst still in the womb) is that the disease is entirely preventable. If every pregnant woman had a blood test taken for syphilis at least once in pregnancy, and if every woman with a positive test was treated with penicillin injections, 'congenital' syphilis would disappear. In fact, in the developed nations, 'congenital' syphilis is increasingly rare, but it does occur. It should not.

Today, the chances of curing early syphilis, that is syphilis in the first or second stage, are excellent. And even in the third stage, the disease can be arrested, although not cured.

The discovery of penicillin, and of the other antibiotics, has completely changed the outlook. But it is not enough for an infected person to receive a full course of penicillin, he or she must also be prepared to have blood tests made at periodic intervals to make sure that a relapse does not occur. Because of the gross damage which syphilis may cause to a person's body and mind, the follow-up has to be even more meticulous than that following treatment for gonorrhoea.

Early infectious syphilis is completely curable if adequate doses of penicillin are given to keep a high blood level of the drug continuously for a period of 10 to 14 days. This

70

means that a man or a woman who has syphilis must have daily injections for at least 14 days, or using a larger dose, must have injections twice weekly for three weeks. If the patient is unable to be given penicillin because of an allergy to the drug, one of the other antibiotics is chosen.

Following treatment the patient is examined and blood tests are taken every month for six months, and then again at nine months and twelve months, after the initial treatment. If the tests are negative by the end of the year, the patient is considered cured.

If syphilis is not detected until the end of, or after, the secondary stage, the treatment is the same, but the follow-up tests are made every two months for the first year, and then every three months for a second year.

In both early infective, and later latent syphilis, the blood tests may show the need for further injections of penicillin.

Obviously the complexity of the follow-up demands that a person who has developed syphilis must cooperate in his treatment, for unless he does in the early stages, he may infect others; and in the later stages he is a danger to himself.

# 5

# Moses,
# Columbus
# and venereal disease

It is probable that sexually transmitted diseases have existed
for as long as humans have copulated, but it must be
admitted that the origins of the two main sexually transmitted diseases, gonorrhoea and syphilis, are obscure.
According to an eminent venereologist of the nineteenth
century, the Frenchman, Philippe Ricord, the first sentence
of the Bible should have been 'In the beginning, God
created the heavens, the earth, man and venereal diseases.'

Gonorrhoea, or a venereal disease which was remarkably
similar, is recorded in the Bible, where some of the earliest
public health measures to prevent its spread are reported.
Some time, about 3000 B.C., the Israelites, under Moses,
made war on the Midianites, to avenge themselves for some
real or imagined insult to them and to their God. In the
first recorded account of a supernatural excuse being used
to justify a war, the aim of which was to destroy the
enemy's economic strength, the Israelites prospered, and
won. As part of their victory they killed all the surviving
male Midianites, and took the women and children captive,
burning the Midianite villages and confiscating their herds
of cattle and flocks of sheep. It was an utterly ruthless,
vicious attack by one primitive tribe on another. They
brought their booty, including the human booty, to a concentration camp on the plain of Moab near Jericho. It
appears that the Israelites, flush with victory, copulated with

72

the Midianite women, for there was 'a plague amongst the congregation of the Lord'. Moses ordered that every Midianite woman 'that had known man by lying with him' should be killed, and every Israelite man who had copulated should be isolated 'outside the camp' for a period of seven days. It is interesting to note that infection with gonorrhoea usually shows itself within seven days of intercourse with an infected partner.

Oddly, gonorrhoea is not identifiable in Greek or Roman literature, nor does any medieval literature suggest any great concern. Perhaps the disease was so common that it was considered normal. Perhaps, as disease at that time was considered to be due to an act of God because of man's sin, it may have been thought not worth recording. In England by the twelfth century, there was some concern about the disease, and London brothel-keepers were forbidden to supply clients with women who suffered from 'the perilous infirmity of burning'. The term burning was an abbreviation of the Norman-French name for gonorrhoea 'hot piss' or 'la chaude pisse'. The current popular name for gonorrhoea – the clap – only became fashionable about two centuries later, by which time with a relaxation of sexual morality, the disease had become widespread.

By this time, too, syphilis had appeared in Europe to complicate the picture, and for the next 300 years, until 1793, the two diseases were considered to be two different manifestations of a single 'venereal' disease. In part this confusion was increased by the well-known and respected physician John Hunter, who in 1767, 'proved' that the two conditions were one. Hunter believed that the clinical appearance of the disease depended on where the poison was inoculated. If it entered the urethra, the victim developed

73

gonorrhoea; if it infected the penis, the victim developed a syphilitic ulcer. To prove his point he took some pus from a patient who had gonorrhoea and placed it in his urethra. Within seven days he had developed gonorrhoea, and within a month he had developed the skin rash of syphilis. The proof was there – syphilis and gonorrhoea were the same disease. It was of course, no proof at all, for the pus had contained the germs which cause gonorrhoea, *Neisseria gonorrhoeae*, and those which cause syphilis, the *Treponema pallidum*. Unfortunately, Hunter was so eminent, and his views so respected, that his findings were accepted, and further progress was delayed until 1793, when Benjamin Bell in Edinburgh identified that there were two diseases. Unfortunately for John Hunter the syphilis he had acquired led to illness in his last years and eventually to his death. Benjamin Bell was more cautious. He inoculated medical students, and proved that there were two separate sexually transmitted diseases – gonorrhoea and syphilis. William Wallace, in Dublin about fifteen years later, carried the identification one step further. He proved that the skin rash of syphilis, as well as the initial infection, an ulcer on the penis, was highly infectious. He did this by inoculating patients in the free wards of the hospital in which he worked. So much for the ethics of medical practice at that time! Wallace had one other claim to fame. This is in the treatment of syphilis. At that time the only remedy, which was largely ineffectual (as I mentioned in the last chapter), was to give mercury, either rubbed into the skin or taken by mouth, in the form of 'blue pills'. Mercury, of course is very toxic, as the experience of fish eaters in Minamata Bay in Japan has shown recently. Mercury given to cure syphilis, caused teeth to fall out, kidney damage and mental decay – all of which were attributed to the progress of the disease, not to the treatment. Wallace argued that the salt of another element might be even more successful. He chose to give potassium iodide, which led to the medical students' rhyme:

> 'If you lose your faith in God
> Put your trust in pot. iod!'

Unfortunately the use of potassium iodide in the treatment of syphilis was only marginally better, if at all better, than the use of mercury.

Syphilis is one of a group of diseases called treponematoses, because the organisms which cause them are tiny corkscrew-shaped germs called treponemes. In tropical areas a common treponematosis is yaws. Yaws is spread by bodily – not sexual – contact, in conditions of poor hygiene and infrequent washing. The disease is chronic and large ulcers form over the body. It usually only affects small children and persists for years if it is not treated. In tropical America, another variety of treponematosis, called pinta, develops in primitive people in rural areas. In this disease young persons aged 10 to 25, rather than young children, are affected. Once again the disease is spread by body contact, by rubbing against an infected lesion, and not by sexual intercourse.

Syphilis is the only treponematosis which is spread by sexual intercourse. It is also the only one of the diseases which is a potential killer, but because of the existence of other treponemal diseases its origin is obscure.

Until some five years after the return of Columbus from America, syphilis was unknown in Europe, but after that time, for two centuries, the disease raged, as an epidemic,

75

throughout the continent. Those who believe that the disease was brought back to Europe by Columbus's sailors, claim that America was given to Europe so that the Europeans might plunder it, and later settle their excess populations in its empty lands, and in return America gave Europe a particularly damaging disease. This new disease spread to all parts of the world from its introduction into Barcelona by sailors infected by the Indians of the Isle of Espanola in the Caribbean.

The first description of the disease was by a Portuguese physician, Ruy Diaz de Isla, who worked in Barcelona. He was called to treat some of Columbus' men, who were covered with a pustular skin rash and had snail-track, or serpentine, ulcers on their mouths and throats. He first termed the disease 'Indian measles' because the skin rash resembled measles, but was not exactly like it. Later he called it the 'serpentine disease'. He described it as 'a disease, previously unknown, unseen and undescribed, which first appeared in the city and spread thence throughout the world'. About 15 years after Diaz saw the first cases, the disease was widespread in all European nations, and he wrote a book which he called *A Treatise on the Serpentine Malady*. In this book he wrote: 'It has pleased divine justice to give and send down upon us unknown afflictions, never seen nor recognized nor found in medical books, such as this serpentine disease . . . at the time that the Admiral don Xristoual Colon (Columbus) arrived in Spain, the Catholic sovereigns were in the city of Barcelona. And when they went to give them an account of their voyage and of what they had discovered, immediately the city began to be infected and the aforesaid disease spread as was seen later on through long experience.'

76

# LE BAGAGE.

*Fig. 5/1. Le Bagage, or the camp follower. 'The impedimenta of the Army. Triumph of the high and mighty, Dame Syphilis, Queen of the Fountain of Love' (Lyons, 1539). From Pusey, W. A., 'The History and Epidemiology of Syphilis', 1933. Courtesy of Charles C. Thomas, Publisher, Springfield, Illinois.*

The alternative view of the origin of syphilis is that the treponeme group of diseases existed in Europe (as they did in Africa and America) but were so mild that they were unrecognized. Then in the last decade of the fifteenth century they suddenly became virulent and sexually transmissible.

Whatever the origin, after 1494 syphilis rapidly spread throughout Europe. In the autumn of 1494, Charles VIII of France invaded Italy to seize the throne of Naples. His army consisted of mercenaries, including Spanish mercenaries, and they laid siege to Naples. Accompanying the army, as was the custom, went a collection of female camp followers, known as 'baggages' (Fig. 5/1). The king of Naples had also obtained mercenary soldiers to defend his city, and these included a number of Spanish soldiers. There was little fighting, but much fornication by both armies, and by the spring of 1495 a new plague had affected both the defenders and the attackers. The plague was the serpentine disease of Diaz. The new disease was so severe and so many of his troops were affected, that Charles was forced to abandon his siege and retreat from Italy. With his army he took the new unnamed disease. As the mercenaries returned to their homelands they fornicated on the way, and those they infected spread the new disease. It passed down from man to woman and then to another man and another woman with great rapidity. Sexually transmissible, the new disease was transmitted by frequent fornication with different partners. As the people of each country became infected, each tried to put the blame for the new and terrifying disease on its neighbour. The Italians called it the Spanish disease. The French, who were infected in 1495, called it the Italian or Neapolitan disease. By 1496 the disease was infecting large numbers of people in Germany, France and Switzerland. It reached Holland and Greece in 1496, and England in 1497, where it was called the French disease. In the same year Perkin Warbeck, who claimed to be the Duke of York, had invaded the north of England, from Scotland, with 1400 disreputable followers, and with the support of James IV of Scotland. Amongst these mercenaries were some from Charles' army. The invasion was a failure and the motley regiment was driven back into Scotland. They

78

took with them the new serpentine disease. In Aberdeen the disease took hold so rapidly that by 1497 the town's leaders became dismayed. Recognizing that the disease was spread by sexual intercourse, they published a regulation in which they ordered 'all light women to desist from their vice and sin of venery' on pain of being branded. The regulation was ineffective. Sex continued rampant, and by 1507 the authorities of Aberdeen ordered that 'diligent inquisition be taken of all infected persons with this strange sickness of Napolis for the safety of the town'. The infected were ordered 'to keep quiet in their houses'!

By 1500, the disease had spread to Hungary and Russia, and was being taken to India by the Portuguese explorers under Vasco da Gama. It reached China in 1505 and Japan a year later where it was called 'manka bassam' or the Portuguese disease.

The epidemic raged like a bush fire. Because of the virulence of the organisms, or the lack of resistance by the people to the new disease, it was viciously severe. The primary lesion was hardly noticed when compared with the secondary lesions, which developed six to eight weeks later. These caused severe illnesses, and often deaths, as the pustular ulcerated skin rashes, and the snail track lesions in the mouth, the throat and the genitals spread unabated. Such evidence as there is suggests that many thousands died. As well as causing death, the skin lesions were highly infectious and even non-sexual contact with an infected person caused the infection to spread. Such was the concern of the people, that the Holy Church was petrified, and a patron saint was appointed to whom victims might pray. By a coincidence he was also the patron saint of France and of Paris. It seemed that the French were to be blamed for the

79

disease, which in a way, was logical, for it was the French king's mercenary army which had started its rapid spread. St. Denis, patron saint of Paris and of France, became the patron saint of the new disease, and in a book published between 1496 and 1500, he is seen standing by and interceding with the Virgin on behalf of pock-marked sufferers from the new plague (Fig. 5/2).

Treatment seemed ineffective, although mercury was used, in the hope that it would help. Prayer also seemed ineffective. The disease continued to spread with increasing severity. In the early years severe ulcerating, pustular rashes on the skin and in the mouth predominated. They were associated with fevers and aching pains deep in the bones. As time passed, the rash became less obvious, but many victims infected earlier developed gummy ulcerated swellings in their bones, which often ate away the cartilage of the palate and nose. By now, too, mercury toxicity was causing baldness and loss of teeth. Bone pains, which were gnawing, and occurred at night, persisted, keeping the victim awake and screaming.

It took over a hundred years for the severity of the disease to moderate, and the pattern seen today to evolve. But during that century, the disease rampaged and together with bubonic plague and enteric fevers laid waste many families.

The name syphilis was first given to the disease in 1530, when Dr. Fracastor, a physician and a poet of Verona in Italy wrote a poem about a young swineherd, called Syphilis, who angered the god, Apollo, by building forbidden altars on a sacred hill. As a punishment Apollo inflicted a terrible disease on him, in which ulcers of the skin, or buboes, were the main feature.

80

*Fig. 5/2. St. Denis, supplicates the Virgin Mary to help a victim of the new disease. (Originally in Grunpeck's book published between 1496 and 1500.) From Pusey, W. A., 'The History and Epidemiology of Syphilis', 1933. Courtesy of Charles C. Thomas, Publisher, Springfield, Illinois.*

'He first wore buboes dreadful to the sight
First felt strange pains, and sleepless passed the night
From him the malady received its name
The neighbouring shepherds catch'd the spreading flame'
So wrote Fracastorius.

The title page of Fracastor's poem reads 'Syphilis sive Morbus Gallicus'. This is translated as 'Syphilis, or the French Disease'. There can be no doubt that Dr. Fracastor had seen several cases of the 'serpentine disease', and he wrote his poem to give it a proper name. As the Italians claimed the disease had been introduced by the French (whom they detested), it seemed a good way, to Fracastor, to give the disease a second name, the French disease. His poem was widely read, and the disease generally acquired the name, syphilis, which had none of the pejorative connotations of the earlier names. It has been called syphilis ever since, a sad tribute to a sacrilegious swineherd.

The alternative name, the great-pox, which was chosen to distinguish it from the other epidemic – the small-pox – was introduced in England some time in the sixteenth century, because of the resemblance in the two diseases, of skin lesions which pocked the skin with sores and ulcers. But because the painful symptoms and the number of deaths from syphilis were so much more severe than those of small-pox, it was given the name of the great-pox. By the eighteenth century, the great-pox had become the common term for syphilis. It had, in general, been shortened to 'the pox', which is what it is called today. A students' song about 'The Good Ship Venus' records that one of the sailors 'caught the syph. at Tenerife, the pox in the Canaries'. He was clearly a lusty sailor.

Throughout its recorded history, the main cause of the spread of the disease has been casual fornication, usually with prostitutes. Consequently, travellers, soldiers and sailors have been particularly at risk, as were the rakes and dandies of eighteenth-century England, whose promiscuity was neither in doubt nor unheralded. However, syphilis can affect a bishop or a 'baggage' and neither kings nor the rulers of the earth have been spared. There is good evidence that Henry VIII's inability to have a healthy child and the mental disturbances of his later years were due to syphilis acquired in his youth.

By the nineteenth century, a revulsion from the overt sexuality of the two earlier centuries had made venereal disease one of the unmentionable matters, in Britain at least, together with women's legs and breasts. This in no way reduced the incidence nor spread of the sexually transmitted disease, which in a man was considered indiscreet, or perhaps degrading, but in a woman was treated as a crime. The double standard towards sexuality, which regrettably persists today, received a majestic reinforcement from mid-Victorian paternalistic, authoritarian 'morality'.

Despite the widespread prevalence of syphilis, no documentation was made of its frequency, except amongst soldiers. In the mid-nineteenth century, rates of 70 to 120 per 1000 men were reported from the armies of the U.S.A., Britain, Prussia and France. By the onset of World War I, the rates had decreased 20–45 per cent, as the conspiracy of secrecy and the punitive attitude of authority towards infected men diminished. During this period, too, education was becoming more widespread, particularly of the working classes, who are recorded as having two or three times the chance of contracting the disease, although this statistic may be artificial as many wealthier syphilitics were treated by private doctors, and the disease was never reported to the public health authorities.

The available evidence suggests that the decline in the number of new cases of syphilis and gonorrhoea reported each year between 1850 and 1910 was real, and was more related to social factors than to control of the disease, which was rudimentary, or to treatment, which was ineffectual.

In 1910, for the first time, a treatment was devised which had the possibility of curing syphilis. This was Ehrlich's 'magic bullet', or Salvarsan. Salvarsan, which was an arsenical and given by injection, seemed to offer a cure. At the same time the development of microscopy had enabled doctors to diagnose the disease early, and a blood test had been devised by Wassermann to detect those in whom the clinical signs of syphilis had disappeared, but who still had the disease. It appeared that a new, and more scientific, period in the management of syphilis was about to begin.

The situation with gonorrhoea was different. Although the organism causing the disease had been identified by Neisser in 1879 (hence the official name of the organism, *Neisseria gonorrhoeae*), and from that date gonorrhoea could be easily diagnosed, in men at least, no effective treatment was available until sulphonamides and later penicillin were introduced in the 1940s. And with the ready availability of penicillin many people believed that both syphilis and gonorrhoea would be eliminated rapidly.

It has not worked out that way, at all. In fact in the last decade, in all western nations, there has been an upsurge in the incidence of both syphilis and gonorrhoea. In the U.S.A., for example, infectious syphilis is now more common than poliomyelitis, tuberculosis and the other infectious diseases which, not so long ago, were considered a threat to mankind.

It is difficult to determine exactly how common the sexually transmitted diseases are, as a large number of infected people are treated by private doctors who feel they have neither the duty to report, nor do they have the wish to embarrass a paying patient by reporting the disease to the public health authorities. Yet if this new epidemic is to be controlled, the names of all infected persons must be notified, so that their sexual partner or partners can be contacted, before they in turn infect other people. The purpose of notifying the public health authorities is not to embarrass, or to punish the individual, but to prevent the disease from spreading. It is a public health matter, not a moral matter.

The most accurate study of the prevalence of syphilis in the population of a nation was made by testing the blood of all men, usually aged 18 to 35, who were drafted into the U.S.A. armed forces in World War II. From these data, it was estimated by Drs. Parran and Vonderlehr that 24 people in every 1000 alive in the United States in 1942 had syphilis, although in most the disease had been treated and was non-infectious.

In most western nations from which accurate data are available, the largest number of new cases of syphilis occurred in the war years, reaching the peak in 1945–6 with demobilization. A dramatic fall occurred between 1946 and 1950. From then until the early 1960s the number of new cases reported declined slightly. Although many cases were not reported, there is evidence that the decline was real (Fig. 5/3). Not all experts agree with this statement. Several have pointed out that the decline in the reporting of numbers of cases of syphilis coincided with the gross misuse by doctors of penicillin and other antibiotics. From the time when antibiotics became readily available, which occurred about 1950, penicillin and, later, the other antibiotics, were given increasingly in inadequate doses to treat trivial diseases, including viral diseases which do not respond to the drugs.

85

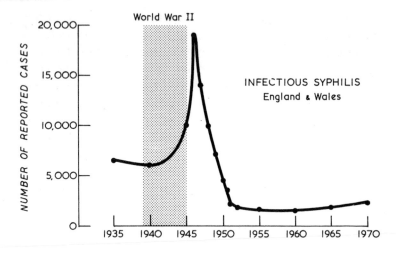

*Fig. 5/3. The decline in the incidence of syphilis since 1946.*

There is a distinct possibility that antibiotics, used in this way, masked the clinical signs of syphilis but did not eliminate the disease which may be smouldering at the moment in many people. If this is so, a rise in the incidence of late syphilis may occur in the 1970s. This potentially serious event could be avoided if every man and woman who has had casual sexual intercourse made sure that he, or she, has a blood test to detect latent syphilis. From the early 1960s, particularly in the U.S.A., with the unnecessary trauma of the U.S. involvement in the Vietnamese war, the incidence of reported syphilis has risen. This rise has also occurred in western nations, but has been less marked. The possible reasons for this increase will be discussed later.

The world total of persons infected with syphilis is astonishing. A committee of UNESCO estimated that in 1969 'there are now in the world 20 to 50 million cases

86

of venereal syphilis'. It is likely that this is an underestimate because of under-reporting.

The present situation with regard to gonorrhoea is more disturbing. The World Health Organization calculates that ten cases of gonorrhoea occur for every case of syphilis, which means that currently there may be between 200 million and 500 million cases annually. The disease has reached world-wide epidemic proportions. As with syphilis, official figures must be treated with reserve, for in most nations, patients with gonorrhoea seek treatment from private physicians and the disease is not reported. The integrity of private doctors in reporting gonorrhoea varies from country to country. This factor, more than any other is the probable explanation for the apparently high incidence in Sweden, in 1970, of 425 infections per 100,000 population and the apparently low incidence in Portugal of 25 per 100,000 of the population.

In all western nations reporting, the rise in gonorrhoea has been startling. In England and Wales, the increase between 1960 and 1970 was 65 per cent, and the peak incidence of the war years has been exceeded. This rise has occurred disproportionately amongst women, and especially amongst women under the age of 25 (Fig. 5/4). Perhaps the most spectacular rise has been in the U.S.A., where the number of reported cases rose from 270,000 in 1960 to 450,000 in 1970. The real number of cases is much higher. A survey in the U.S.A. in 1968 by Dr. Mackenzie-Pollock showed that 80 per cent of cases of gonorrhoea were treated by private doctors, but only one case in nine was reported to the health authorities. This suggests that in 1960 over 1 million cases occurred and by 1970 the number of new cases of gonorrhoea had risen to over 2 million. There is

87

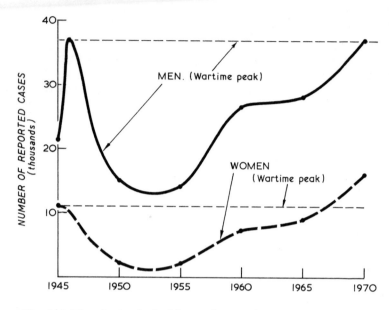

*Fig. 5/4. The rise in the incidence of gonorrhoea in the United Kingdom since 1955.*

also evidence that increases have occurred in most developing nations, although accurate data are not usually available. Against this trend are reports from the U.S.S.R., Eastern Europe and China. In these nations, the incidence of gonorrhoea per 100,000 of the population seems to be falling.

In all nations reporting statistics of sexually transmitted diseases, more and more teenagers are becoming infected with gonorrhoea, and recent surveys in Western nations show that over 55 per cent of all cases occur in people under the age of 25. Amongst this age group between three and five times as many men as women are infected. Before

88

this statistic leads to complacency amongst women it must be remembered that gonorrhoea in a woman is much more serious to her own health, and to the public health, than it is in a man, as more than one woman in three who has gonorrhoea has no knowledge that she is infected.

The rise in incidence of gonorrhoea in the past ten years is due to greater sexual activity by young people, and particularly by young girls. Moralists may deplore this, but the facts are that it is occurring, and unless there is a sudden dramatic change in sexual attitudes it is likely to persist. Rather than uttering plaintive, platitudinous prophesies about moral decay, the moralists should be bending their energies to reducing the effects of this greater sexuality amongst young people. These effects include the spread of sexually transmissible diseases and an increase in extra-marital, unwanted pregnancies. Both could be reduced by better education about human sexuality and about sexually transmitted diseases, by removing the stigma of seeking medical help if the young person catches gonorrhoea or syphilis, so that he or she seeks medical aid, at once, without fear or shame. This demands that moralists treat the sexually transmitted diseases as infectious diseases, like every other infectious disease. Medically, syphilis and gonorrhoea should be managed in the same way as measles, poliomyelitis or food poisoning. The second effect of increased sexuality, that of unwanted pregnancy, could be reduced by better education and by the better distribution of contraceptives which should be freely available. In fact if condoms were freely available to all adolescents and it was the fashion to use one when having casual coitus, the incidence of gonorrhoea would decline. Today in the English-speaking nations, gonorrhoea is more likely to be contracted by fornicating with a friend than by copulating with a prostitute. A survey in the U.S.A. showed that 20 per cent of prostitutes had gonorrhoea and 2 per cent had infectious syphilis. In the nations of Europe, where prostitution is under stricter control and brothels are usual, the infection rate amongst professional prostitutes is said to be lower. Amongst promiscuous males and females it seems far higher.

Homosexual men appear to be an increasing source of new cases, both of syphilis and gonorrhoea. Whether the increase is real or apparent is not certain. In Britain this is because alterations in the law in 1967, which made homosexuality between consenting adult males no longer a crime, made it possible for homosexuals to seek treatment without fear of prosecution; but it may also be a real increase. Since between five and 10 per cent of all males are homosexual, and since many homosexuals are promiscuous, it is not unrealistic to expect that many cases of venereal disease will occur amongst homosexuals. It is not known whether homosexual promiscuity is due to childhood emotional disturbances which prevent the man from forming any lasting relationship with another person, or whether the contempt shown by society, and the penalties it imposes on known homosexuals, are the major factors in homosexual promiscuity. Research in this area is urgently needed.

# 6

# other

# sexually

# transmitted

# diseases

## non-specific urethritis

A disturbing condition affecting men particularly, which appears to be sexually transmitted, has increased in reported numbers in the past two decades in several countries. In England and Wales, for example, 11,500 cases were reported from hospital clinics in 1952; ten years later this had risen to 25,000 and by 1972 to over 50,000. This last figure exceeds that of gonorrhoeal infections of males reported in the same year.

The condition is called non-specific urethritis, because no specific cause, such as gonorrhoea, trichomoniasis (see page 94), chemical irritation, or anxiety-induced irritation, can be found.

About 10 to 30 days after sexual intercourse, usually with a casual partner, the man discovers that he has a discharge from his urethra, which may be clear or purulent. When he urinates, the passage of the urine along his urethra causes pain, although often this is only mild. Occasionally, the symptoms are more severe. The man develops bladder pain and an urgent and frequent need to pass urine. If he seeks medical examination he should avoid passing urine for at least two hours before seeing the doctor. The doctor

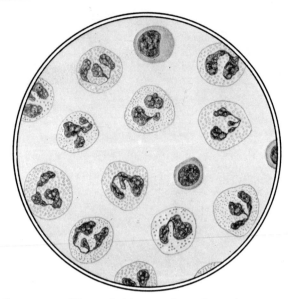

*Fig. 6/1. Non-specific urethritis seen through a microscope (compare with Fig. 3/3).*

may massage his penis along the urethra, to express a bead of pus, or it may be present without the need to do this.

The pus is placed on a slide and examined under a microscope, and usually 'cultured' as I described in the diagnosis of gonorrhoea. Neither the slide, nor the culture, shows any organisms and all that is found are numerous pus cells, which are merely special white blood cells (Fig. 6/1).

It will be appreciated that clinically the disease is identical with gonorrhoea in its early stages, and the diagnosis can only be made by excluding gonorrhoea and other specific infections. For this reason, and also because non-specific urethritis can have unpleasant complications, it is essential that a man who develops painful urination and a urethral discharge seeks a medical opinion and has the appropriate treatment when a diagnosis has been made.

The complications involve the spread of the causative organism – which is probably a virus-like agent – to the male bladder or to his prostate gland. If the bladder becomes infected, the man complains of severe pain, especially when he passes urine, which he wants to do all too often, and is often unable to do because of the pain. If the organism spreads into the prostate gland it causes discomfort deep in the pelvis. Sometimes the spread is without symptoms, but from the warm security of the prostate gland, the disease may affect distant organs. In fact, a peculiar group of symptoms seems to follow untreated non-specific urethritis. These are conjunctivitis, urethritis and painful swellings of several of the bigger joints, a form of acute arthritis. The conjunctivitis and urethritis start days, or weeks, after exposure to infection, and settle quite quickly. The arthritis starts rather more slowly and persists. There may be associated fever and a feeling of being vaguely ill. There is reason to believe that the group of symptoms – called a syndrome – is due to an allergic reaction to persistence of the organism in the body, probably in the prostate gland. The syndrome, first described by a Dr. Reiter, and subsequently called Reiter's syndrome, settles after a few months, and the joints usually recover, but further attacks are usual, and these may lead to permanent damage and deformities of the affected joints.

These insidious developments are largely (but not completely) avoided by adequate treatment of the initial infection. Treatment is to avoid all sexual intercourse until the symptoms have disappeared, and for four to six weeks after that. In addition antibiotics, especially 'broad-spectrum' antibiotics, such as tetracycline or one of its derivatives, are prescribed in an appropriate dose. During treatment and for four to six weeks after its completion, alcohol should be avoided as it seems to increase the resistance to cure.

Because non-specfic urethritis is infectious, all sexual partners of the infected man should be contacted, examined and if infected, treated, or the disease will continue to spread. This is most important, as there is no certain cure for non-specific urethritis' unpleasant sequel – Reiter's syndrome.

Non-specific urethritis also occurs in women, but has fewer sequels, and Reiter's syndrome is uncommon. This is because a woman's urethra is shorter and she has no prostate gland in which to harbour the organism. However, as she may infect subsequent partners it is important that she is examined, tested and treated.

# trichomoniasis

The problems of non-specific urethritis are much more common in men than in women, but women tend to develop vaginal infestation with a tiny parasite, *Trichomonas vaginalis*, with particular frequency. The true incidence of *Trichomonas vaginalis* in a population is unknown, but it has been estimated to be present in the vaginas of between 10 and 20 per cent of women in the reproductive years of 15 to 49. One calculation suggests that at any one time over two million women in Britain have vaginal infestation with trichomoniasis, although most of these women have no symptoms and do not know that they are infected. By contrast a survey of 997 unselected virgins, aged 12 to 14 showed that only two per cent had trichomoniasis. This is the reason

94

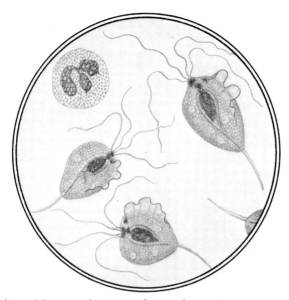

*Fig. 6/2. Trichomonads seen under a microscope.*

for including the disease amongst the sexually transmitted diseases.

The parasite, which can only be seen through a microscope, is about 20μ in length, is globular in shape and has four moving threads at the front end, called flagellae, because of their whip-like action in propelling the organism. Along its body from its head-end, an undulating membrane stretches, which waves as the creature moves (Fig. 6/2). It is about the size of a pus cell. Although the trichomonad usually inhabits the vagina, it occasionally enters the urethra and its associated extensions (which you may remember, are called Skene's ducts), the bladder and Bartholin's gland.

Contrary to the popular belief that the vagina is a smooth-walled well-lubricated tube, at least during sexual

95

intercourse, it is, in fact, a most complex structure. Normally its two sides lie in touch with each other, and the wall itself is raised into complicated folds and clefts like a curtain of thick velvet. The importance of this concept is that the *Trichomonas vaginalis* organisms can lodge deep in clefts where they obtain all the nourishment they want. In this warm, nutritious, protected environment they multiply.

There is increasing evidence that *Trichomonas vaginalis* is largely a sexually transmitted disease. As I mentioned, it is unusual to find it in virgins, and it is found more often in women who have had sexual intercourse. A typical story is for a girl to complain of vaginal itch, with some vaginal discharge, which may or may not be profuse, which began within 7 to 21 days of starting sexual intercourse. The itch is usually more severe than the discharge, and tenderness may make further coitus very painful or impossible. In severe infections, the discharge is profuse and offensive. The vagina is intensely tender, and the vulva is reddened, swollen and inflamed, so that coitus is impossible, urination painful, walking uncomfortable, and sitting a misery. Investigation of the discharge shows the presence of actively moving trichomonads, and smears taken from the male partner's urethra show where the infection came from. In men, the male urethra, or its extensions, are often infected, but in most cases the man has no symptoms. However in some men a urethritis occurs, and statistics suggest that about 10 to 20 per cent of cases of non-gonorrhoeal urethritis are due to infection by *Trichomonas vaginalis*. The importance of these observations is that when a woman is diagnosed as having *Trichomonas vaginalis*, both she and any sexual partners she may have must be treated, as between 30 and 70 per cent of the partners will also have the infection.

96

*Trichomonas vaginalis* is said to be more frequent amongst prostitutes than puritans, negroes than whites, amongst pregnant than non-pregnant women, and amongst women in the developing nations than amongst affluent women of the rich nations. As well as this, investigations show that between 40 and 60 per cent of women with infectious gonorrhoea also harbour trichomonads in their vaginas. It is this additional infection which mainly accounts for the vaginal discharge these women complain about, for as was recorded earlier, the gonococcus cannot infect the vagina of an adult.

Although 10 to 20 per cent, or more, of women of reproductive age have trichomoniasis, in the majority, the parasites live in harmony with the woman who unsuspectingly harbours them, and only cause symptoms from time to time. It is possible that frequent coitus may stimulate them, or that they cause symptoms only when the environment of the vagina changes for one reason or another.

In recent years the development of a drug, metronidazole, has revolutionized the treatment of trichomoniasis. The drug is effective when given by mouth, and no vaginal preparations are needed. But as it is specific for trichomoniasis, a diagnosis must be made before it is prescribed. This is done by taking a specimen of the discharge from inside the vagina. If the discharge is mixed with a drop of salt solution on a warmed slide, the parasite can be seen moving across the field, when looked at down a microscope. This method is useful if the parasite is seen, but its absence is not evidence that the patient has not got trichomoniasis. To be sure, a specimen of the discharge is added to a test-tube containing a substance (Feinberg-Whittington medium) in which it grows excellently. This is incubated for 48 to 72

97

hours, when specimens of the solution are examined micro-
scopically for trichomonads.

The treatment with metronidazole, which commercially
is called Flagyl, is to give one tablet three times a day for
7 to 10 days, to the infected person and his, or her, partner.
Recently a simpler treatment which seems almost as effective has been introduced in England. In this new method
the whole dose of metronidazole is given at one go. The
couple take 5 or 10 tablets at one time and do not have
to remember to take the tablets over the ten day period,
which may be an advantage.

A man is usually cured with a single course (or the 'one-
shot' treatment) but trichomonads tend to persist in a
woman because of the nature of her vagina. For this reason
she can only be sure she is cured if further tests are made
on swabs taken from her vagina just after her next menstrual period (and preferably after her next three menstrual
periods) and these tests fail to show any trichomonads.

However, the cure rate is high. Over 90 per cent of
infected women are cured with a single course of the drug,
and the other 10 per cent are cured if a second treatment
is given using a higher dose.

# candidiasis
# (or vaginal moniliasis, or vaginal thrush)

Infection of the vagina by a fungus is even more common
amongst women of the reproductive age, than infection with

the parasite, *Trichomonas vaginalis.* The usual infection is by the fungus which causes 'thrush' in babies' mouths, and which, in women, is called vaginal candidiasis, or moniliasis. The sociological factors which increase the chance of infection with trichomoniasis apply also to candidiasis, but there are a few additional factors. Candidiasis is often found in diabetic women, and is particularly common in pregnancy. It may also cause symptoms after a woman has been given a course of penicillin, or some other antibiotic. A good deal of discussion has taken place to decide if candidiasis is more likely to occur amongst women on 'the pill', and although it does appear to be more common, the evidence is by no means certain. It is better to be protected against an unwanted pregnancy by taking 'the pill', than to worry about the chance of developing vaginal candidiasis. Without contraception pregnancy is likely to follow, and pregnancy is a particular stimulus to the appearance of vaginal thrush. 'The pill' is the most efficient of all the available contraceptives, and in most cases will be the first choice. But if a woman has had candidiasis previously, she may choose to have an intra-uterine device inserted into her uterus. The method does not give such good protection against unwanted pregnancy, but is still pretty efficient. Alternatively her partner can use a condom, whilst she uses a spermicidal vaginal cream each time they have sexual intercourse.

Statistics of the incidence of vaginal candidiasis suggest that about one woman in every four, mainly of reproductive age, harbours the fungus in her vagina, but in only 5 to 30 per cent of women does it produce symptoms. In the other cases the fungus lives quietly and without symptoms in the moist vagina. Amongst virgins the incidence is about 3 to

99

7 per cent, a quarter of that found amongst sexually active women.

*Candida albicans*, so called to distinguish it from other forms of thrush, is a yeast-like organism, which grows particularly well in a moist atmosphere, especially when the secretions contain carbohydrate. This is the reason for its growth in pregnancy and in diabetic women. If bacteria are present its growth tends to be suppressed, which is why it is likely to grow when a woman has taken antibiotics to eliminate bacterial infection somewhere in her body.

The main symptoms in women are a thickish, whitish, vaginal discharge, which is often profuse, and is associated with vaginal and vulval itching. The itch can be quite intolerable and is noticed particularly at night. If the woman scratches herself to relieve the itch, her vulva may becomes very sore and swollen. Occasionally scratching introduces secondary infection, and small, exquisitely painful ulcers result, with increased swelling of the labia around her vulva.

In men, who are infected by sexual partners who harbour the fungus, the glans penis, and the foreskin, become itchy. Occasionally the condition leads to a urethral discharge. A few men develop small superficial ulcers on the glans penis two days, or so, after sexual intercourse. These are very itchy and are associated with a burning feeling over the glans penis.

The diagnosis can be easy, or rather difficult. In a typical case, a specimen of the discharge, placed on a glass slide and stained appropriately, shows the fungus as long threads with bulbous protuberances when viewed down a microscope (Fig. 6/3). In other cases the discharge has to be inoculated into a culture medium, and incubated, before the

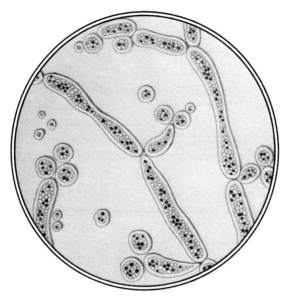

*Fig. 6/3.* Candida albicans *seen through a microscope.*

fungus can be found. When the woman complains of very little vaginal discharge but a very itchy vulva, tiny scrapings of skin taken painlessly from the vulva, and stained, may show *Candida albicans.*

In most cases of vaginal, or vulval infection, treatment is easy. The patient places a tablet of a substance called nystatin, high up in her vagina, morning and evening for 14 days and then once daily at bedtime for a further 14 days. She must put the tablets in her vagina even if she is menstruating, and indeed, it is particularly important to use the tablets over this time. If she has a vulval itch, a cream containing nystatin is used. Her male partner, particularly if he has an itchy glans penis, also uses the nystatin cream twice daily.

101

A few women are not so easily treated. In them the fungus causes such a marked reaction that it is difficult to use the pessaries, and the vulva may be so swollen and painful that sitting and sleeping are impossible. When this occurs, the woman needs to be admitted to hospital, so that soothing soaks can be applied to the inflamed vulva, and the vagina can be painted with swabs dipped into the blue-coloured 'gentian violet'. This treatment is messy, but effective, when the more specific treatment using nystatin tablets is not possible.

Relapse may occur, and when possible follow-up tests should be made over a period of about three months. If thrush is again detected, a further course of nystatin vaginal tablets is needed.

The main reason for recurrence and for the difficulty of cure is delay. If the woman seeks medical diagnosis and treatment soon after she develops symptoms of vulval or vaginal itch, or a vaginal discharge, cure is much quicker. Delay leads to pain and makes the condition more difficult to cure.

Unfortunately, many parents feel that the genitals are organs to be ashamed of, and are unable to talk to their children about sexuality so that many girls who develop candidiasis are afraid or ashamed to admit it. Either they feel guilty that they have 'caught a venereal disease', or that their parents, or their doctor, will abuse them for having had sexual intercourse. Instead of seeking early treatment, they delay, and the condition gets worse. This also applies to girls who develop trichomoniasis.

Luckily, we are entering a period of greater enlightenment towards sexuality, and less hypocrisy about sexual intercourse. As sex education increases in schools, and as parents are better able to talk about sex to their children, the misery caused by minor sexually transmissible disease will diminish.

# genital warts

Genital warts, which occur on the penis, on the vulva or around the anus have been known, and written about since the days of ancient Greece. The warts may be single or may be multiple, covering large areas of the skin, and in the case of women, extending into the vagina. They only occur after sexual maturity has been reached, and they have a peak age incidence between the ages of 18 and 24 in men and women. This is also the peak age incidence of gonorrhoea, which suggests that they are spread by sexual intercourse. In men the foreskin, the frenulum, and the lower edge of the glans penis are most frequently affected, whilst in women the warts are most frequently found in the inner surface of the labia majora. The warts arise when a virus enters the skin through an invisible abrasion, which probably occurred during sexual intercourse. However, the virus tends to remain quiet, and the warts only appear about three months after intercourse with a partner who had genital warts. Once the warts begin to grow, they tend to spread, and this spread is increased if an infected woman becomes pregnant.

The warts may spread to the area around the anus, but if they are only found in this area it is suggestive that anal sexual intercourse has taken place. In a study of 60 men and 8 women who had anal warts, Dr. Oriel of London found that 83 per cent of the men and 62 per cent of the women said that they enjoyed anal intercourse.

Apart from looking unsightly, and being slightly irritating, the warts do no harm, but if they are present the individual should obtain treatment.

# chancroid

For completeness, chancroid should be mentioned, for in law, in Britain and Australia at least, together with syphilis and gonorrhoea it forms one of the three legally-named 'venereal diseases'.

Chancroid is a sexually transmitted disease which usually occurs in the tropics, and only rarely in temperate climates. However with increased air travel and movement of people it is now being encountered in many countries.

It is an acute infectious disease of the genitals which is caused by a small organism, called *Haemophilus ducreyi* after its discoverer, Dr. Ducrey, who first identified it in an ulcer on a man's penis, ninety years ago.

Three to seven days after sexual intercourse with an infected partner, the man develops one or more small painful pimples on his penis, or the woman develops them on her labia. Very quickly the pimples grow, become very tender and then break down to form ulcers which have ragged edges and sloughing base. They are soft, bleed easily and are very painful, (you may remember that the primary lesion of syphilis, the chancre, is usually single, has a hard edge and is not painful). The glands in the groin become swollen and may become 'matted' together to form a large red painful swelling (Fig. 6/4).

The diagnosis is relatively easy, and is confirmed by taking a specimen from one of the ulcers and, after staining,

104

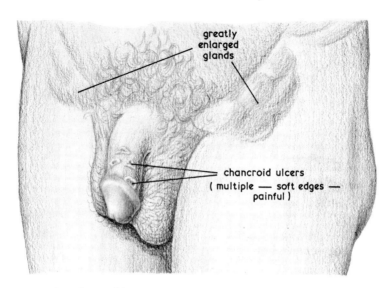

*Fig. 6/4. Chancroid.*

looking down the microscope to find the organisms. In most cases this is unnecessary as the ulcers are fairly typical, and the doctor gives treatment at once.

Treatment is to give sulphonamides, which are most effective in curing chancroid, and have the advantage over the antibiotics that they do not suppress the early signs of syphilis.

An individual infected with chancroid may also be infected, at the same time, with syphilis, so that after curing the chancroid, the patient must report any new lesion on his genitals, or any long-lasting skin rash (by this I mean a rash lasting for more than 14 days), and he should have routine blood tests made for syphilis at monthly intervals for three months.

105

# nine

# points

# for thought

It is worth summarizing the nine most important points of this book.

℘

Unless there is a sudden and remarkable change in attitudes towards sexuality, casual copulation is likely to continue, and to be enjoyed by more and more men and women.

℘

The dangers of casual copulation are that the woman may become pregnant and that both sexes may develop a sexually transmitted disease.

℘

The two most serious sexually transmitted diseases are syphilis and gonorrhoea. The United Nations calculated that, in the world, in 1972, 200 million people were infected with gonorrhoea and 50 million with infectious syphilis, and the numbers are increasing.

℘

Gonorrhoea and syphilis are infectious diseases, which are spread by sexual intercourse, and should be managed like any other infectious disease. This means that to control the 'world-wide epidemic', all those infected should be treated promptly and properly, and all 'contacts' should be traced so that they may be examined and if found to be infected may be treated.

*❧*

Any man, or woman, who develops an ulcer on the genitals, or a discharge from the urethra, and who has had sexual intercourse recently should go to a doctor and have tests made.

*❧*

Any woman, or homosexual man, who has sexual intercourse with a number of partners should go and be examined by a doctor at regular intervals, so that hidden gonorrhoea or syphilis may be detected, and treated.

*❧*

Treatment is not painful, nor difficult, but it does need the cooperation of the infected person.

*❧*

There is nothing to be ashamed about in having become infected with a sexually transmitted disease; after all many eminent men and women have been infected in the past, and may well have been infected recently. What is anti-social, silly and dangerous to the community and to the person, is to avoid going for medical help when the symptoms of the diseases occur.

*❧*

A part of the problem is society's attitude to sexuality. So long as sexual intercourse, outside marriage, continues, and is condemned, and so long as it is considered indecent to talk about the sexually transmitted diseases, so long will they spread and be difficult to control. Education in human sexuality, its delights and its consequences is needed. This should start in primary schools and continue throughout the school years. It should also continue, through the mass media so that all citizens may know their responsibilities, if they develop a venereal disease.

# further

# reading

If any reader wishes to pursue the study of sexually transmitted diseases, the following books and articles in medical
journals may be of interest.

CATERALL, R. D. *A Short Textbook of Venereology*, English
University Press, London, 1965.

GJESTLAND, T. 'Oslo Study of Untreated Syphilis', *Acta.
Dermatol. et Venerol.* 35 Suppl. 1955.

KING, A. and NICOL, C. *Venereal Diseases*, 2nd Edn.,
Baillière Tindall, London, 1969.

MACKENZIE-POLLOCK, J. S. 'Physician Reporting of
Venereal Disease in the U.S.', *Brit. J. of Ven. Dis.*, **46**: 114,
1970.

MORTON, R. S. *Sexual Freedom and Venereal Diseases*, Owen,
London, 1971.

PARKER, J. D. J. 'Recent Trends in the Management of
Urethritis', *Medical Gynaecology and Sociology*, **6**: 9, 1972.

PLATTS, W. M. *A Handbook of Venereal Diseases*, 2nd edn.,
Peryer, Christchurch, New Zealand, 1974.

PUSEY, W. A. *The History and Epidemiology of Syphilis*.
Thomas, Springfield, Illinois, 1933.

U.S. Department of Health, Education and Welfare,
*Syphilis – A Synopsis*. Washington, 1967.

World Health Organization. *Gonococcal Infections* (Technical
Report 262), Geneva, 1963. *Venereal Infections and Treponematosis* (Technical Report 190), Geneva, 1960.

# Index

Anatomy,
    female genital, 23–33
    male genital, 34–40
Antenatal blood tests for syphilis, 68
Armed forces and V.D., 16, 83
Arthritis, 93
Attitudes to V.D., 12–13, 19, 21

Bartholin's glands, 28
Bell, Benjamin, 74
Blood tests for syphilis, 52–3, 55, 67–8, 71, 84

*Candida albicans*, 100
Candidiasis,
    diagnosis, 100–1
    incidence, 98–9
    symptoms, 100
    treatment, 101–2
Carunculae myrtiformes, 28
Cervix uteri, 31–2
Chancre, 55, 56
Chancroid,
    diagnosis, 104–5
    symptoms, 104
    treatment, 105
Circumcision, 36–7
Clitoris, 25
Columbus, Christopher, 75–6
Contact tracing, 20
'Crown of Venus', 59

Denmark, V.D. in, 17

Fallopian tubes (*see* Oviducts)
'Follow-up',
    of gonorrhoea, 49–50
    of syphilis, 52–3, 71

Foreskin, 35–7, 103
Frenulum, 25, 36, 37, 103
Fungus, vaginal (*see* Candidiasis)

Genital warts, 103–4
Glans penis (*see* Penis)
Gonococcus (*see* *Neisseria gonorrhoeae*)
Gonorrhoea,
    complications in men, 37, 39, 43–4
    complications in women, 45–6, 50
    diagnosis of, 47–8
    history of, 42, 72–3
    and homosexuals, 17–18, 47
    incidence rising, 13–15
    numbers of people infected, 11, 42
    rectal, 46–7
    'silent', 15, 50
    symptoms of, 43–4
    treatment of, 48–50
Gumma, 65

*Haemophilus ducreyi*, 104
'High-risk' groups, 15–17
Homosexuals and V.D., 17–18, 47, 56, 90
Human mobility and V.D., 15–16
Hunter, John, 73–4
Hymen (maidenhead), 26–8

'Indian measles', 76

Labia majora, 24
Labia minora, 24–5

Maidenhead (*see* Hymen)
Masturbation, 14, 36, 37
    female, 25
Mercury and syphilis, 62–3, 74, 80
Migrant workers and V.D., 15–16
Moniliasis (*see* Candidiasis)

*Neisseria gonorrhoeae*, 41, 42, 74, 84
Non-specific urethritis (*see* Urethritis, non-specific)

'Oslo experiment', 62–7
Ovaries, 33
Oviducts (Fallopian tubes), 32–3

'Package' holidays and V.D., 15–16
Penicillin and V.D., 48–50, 70–1
Penis, 34–7
Potassium iodide in treatment of syphilis, 75
Prepuce (*see* Foreskin)
Probenecid, use with penicillin, 49
Prostate gland, 39
Prostitutes and V.D., 16, 48, 82, 90

Reiter's syndrome, 93–4
Retroversion of the uterus, 32

Salvarsan (Ehrlich's 'magic bullet'), 63, 84
'Serpentine disease', 76, 78, 82
Sexual permissiveness and V.D., 13–14, 16
Sexuality, 'double-standard' of, 14, 83
Skene's ducts, 25, 37
Stricture (of urethra), 44–5
Sweden and V.D., 16, 87
Syphilis,
    blood tests for, 52–3, 55, 67–8, 71, 84

congenital, 67–70
diagnosis of, 51–3
history of, 75–84
and homosexuals, 56
late, 61, 65–7
latent, 61
numbers of people infected, 11, 84–6
primary, 37, 51, 54, 56, 57–8
rectal, 56
secondary, 58–61
treatment, 70–1
untreated, 62–7
Syphilitic warts, 60–1

Tabes dorsalis (late spinal syphilis), 66–7
Testicles (testes), 39–40
*Treponema pallidum*, 52, 53–4, 74
Treponematoses, 75
*Trichomonas vaginalis*, 94–5
Trichomoniasis,
    diagnosis, 95
    incidence, 94, 97
    latent, 94, 97
    symptoms, 96
    treatment, 97–8
Thrush, vaginal (*see* Cadidiasis)

Urethra,
    female, 25
    male, 37
Urbanization and V.D., 18
Urethritis, non-specific,
    diagnosis, 92
    incidence, 91
    treatment, 93–4
U.K., V.D. in, 87
Urethra, female, 25
    male, 37–9
U.S.A., V.D. in, 84, 85, 86, 87

U.S.S.R., V.D. in, 20, 88
Uterus, 30–2

Vagina, 28–30
Vaginal thrush (*see* Candidiasis)
    moniliasis (*see* Candidiasis)
V.D. Clinics, 13
V.D. and homosexuals, 17–18, 47,
    56, 90
V.D., incidence, 11, 86–8
    lack of research into, 22, 90

sociological aspects of, 13–22
under-reporting of, 84–5, 87
Vulva, 24

Wallace, William, 74–5
Warts, genital, 103–4
    syphilitic, 60–1
Wassermann, 84
World Health Organization and
    V.D., 11, 18, 87

Yaws, 75